Demonology for the Global Church

GLOBAL LIBRARY

One may easily dismiss *Demonology for the Global Church* as mere sensationalism based on the title, but that would be to succumb to the attitude of split-level Christianity that Scott MacDonald seeks to address. If one is willing to invest the time and effort to open the book, one is treated to a masterful, well-researched study on the topics of demons, demoniacs, and spiritual warfare that bridges the biblical world and the modern realities. MacDonald explores the major passages in Scripture with a host of Western and Majority World biblical scholars, theologians, and missiologists through the Reformation into the modern world as dialogue partners, providing readers with an objective and rational framework to address demonology in the twenty-first century context. Readers will come to understand that demons, their influence, and spiritual warfare are extant through human history and global in breadth. Whether one be a scholar, pastor, or missionary, this book makes a significant contribution in bringing to light the impact of the spirit realm and spiritual warfare on the material world.

Samuel Law, PhD
Associate Professor of Intercultural Studies,
Senior Dean of Academic Affairs,
Singapore Bible College

Demonology for the Global Church is a great resource for biblical and theological instruction on demonology for African institutions and pastors. It serves to correct unhealthy and unbiblical fears, misconceptions, and practices regarding demonic activities.

Emile Masabarakiza
Senior Pastor, Twin Palm Baptist Church, Lusaka, Zambia
Adjunct Professor, Baptist Theological Seminary of Zambia

In this thought-provoking work, Scott MacDonald reminds us that, throughout time and all over the world, various manifestations of malevolent activity have been recognized and reported. However, the topic of demonology has either been ignored or addressed in a way that is not helpful. The result, as he so clearly shows, is a theological and pastoral deficiency. MacDonald provides us with a balanced and hermeneutically sound understanding of this much misunderstood topic. Focusing on the actions of demons found in Scripture, he explores the multicultural ramifications for a biblical-theological demonology.

Because this work celebrates Christ's victory over the demonic realm, it not only forces us to rethink our ideas about demonology, it also confronts our ideas about soteriology, challenges us to consider how we practice Christianity in a rapidly evolving world, and encourages us to grow in multicultural co-operation and cohesion. The challenge is this: If the Bible is not silent on demonology, we should not be either. The clarity of *Demonology for the Global Church* is a valuable and timely contribution to Christian Theology.

Elizabeth W. Mburu, PhD
Langham Literature Regional Coordinator, Africa
Adjunct Professor, Pan Africa Christian University, Nairobi, Kenya

Demonology is a subject often neglected or sensationalized, but *Demonology for the Global Church* firmly establishes a biblical demonology. The approach to demonology presented in this work is unique. It avoids speculation, speaking where Scripture speaks and not speaking where Scripture is silent – as much as is possible. Finally, the importance of biblical demonology to an understanding of biblical soteriology is expounded. Oh, that this book had been available when I first went to Brazil nearly two decades ago! Every missionary and minister should read this book and let it drive them to the Scriptures to discover the demonology of the Bible, the demonology that God revealed to us.

Stan Meador
Church Planter in Brazil

I have recently read several books on demonology that seek to balance the various views in the marketplace, but Scott MacDonald's *Demonology for the Global Church* presents the biblical teaching with sound hermeneutics. MacDonald is cognizant of global perspectives, but he is more concerned about biblical truth than a synthesis of views. This work is a must-read for those who seek truth rather than fables.

Reuben Chuga, PhD
Professor of Systematic Theology,
Baptist Theological Seminary, Kaduna, Nigeria

Demonology for the Global Church by Scott MacDonald boldly exposes our disguised spiritual enemy – the demonic host. This book of practical research expounds that demons not only inflict temptation and seduction, but they paralyze us with fear or ignorance of spiritual realities. I recommend this book to anyone who wants to discover the truth about Satan's work and those who desire to plant well-equipped churches that can resist our adversary.

Igor Fedorovych
Director of Evangelism and Church Planting,
Professor of Ecclesiology, Kyiv Theological Seminary
Founder and Pastor, Resurrection Church, Kyiv, Ukraine

Mainstream Evangelicalism in North America largely ignores the issue of demonology. When the subject comes up, it causes immediate discomfort, along with the fear that sensationalism and extra-biblical speculation are about to surface. However, as Scott MacDonald rightly points out in this book, the North American church is guilty of compromise with its culture. The subject of angels and demons is pervasive in Scripture, and the only reason biblically oriented Christians on this continent overlook it is due to the powerful influence of Western anti-supernaturalism. MacDonald does an excellent job of charting a sober-minded course through this issue. He wisely begins with a thorough discussion of hermeneutics, cultural assumptions, and theological method. In his actual material on demons, he eschews speculation and strives to stick to the biblical text. *Demonology for the Global Church* was written in an African context by a North American scholar, and I anticipate that it will be a useful resource for the church on every continent.

Zane Pratt
IMB Vice President,
Assessment/Deployment and Training, Richmond, Virginia, USA
Associate Professor of Christian Missions,
The Southern Baptist Theological Seminary, Louisville, Kentucky, USA

When I read that a portion of a book is adapted from a doctoral dissertation, I assume what I will read is dry, academic, and sometimes irrelevant to daily Christian living. That is not the case with this book. While not sacrificing a strong academic focus, Scott MacDonald offers a needed work that stands on the word of God, recognizes the reality of demonic forces, and challenges us to prepare others for this real battle. He does so with a missiological focus, and he does not shy away from difficult Scripture and debated topics. I will use this book as a text in my course on spiritual warfare in evangelism and missions.

Chuck Lawless, PhD
Dean of Doctoral Studies,
Southeastern Seminary, Wake Forest, North Carolina, USA

A must-read for anyone willing to learn about and study biblical demonology and spiritual warfare, *Demonology for the Global Church* provides an insightful perspective on what demon possession and exorcisms mean for the Christians of the twenty-first century. Scott MacDonald, using excellent biblical analysis, masterfully answers the most important questions in demonological studies and profoundly contributes to the understanding of demon possession and exorcisms in cross-cultural contexts.

Edgar Rac
Demonology and Exorcism Researcher, Edinburgh, Scotland

Demonology for the Global Church

A Biblical Approach in a Multicultural Age

Scott D. MacDonald

GLOBAL LIBRARY

© 2021 Scott D. MacDonald

Published 2021 by Langham Global Library
An imprint of Langham Publishing

www.langhampublishing.org

Langham Publishing and its imprints are a ministry of Langham Partnership

Langham Partnership
PO Box 296, Carlisle, Cumbria, CA3 9WZ, UK
www.langham.org

ISBNs:
978-1-83973-224-9 Print
978-1-83973-484-7 ePub
978-1-83973-485-4 Mobi
978-1-83973-486-1 PDF

Scott D. MacDonald has asserted his right under the Copyright, Designs and Patents Act, 1988 to be identified as the Author of this work.

All rights reserved. No part of this publication may be reproduced, stored in a retrieval system or transmitted, in any form or by any means, electronic, mechanical, photocopying, recording or otherwise, without the prior written permission of the publisher or the Copyright Licensing Agency.

Requests to reuse content from Langham Publishing are processed through PLSclear. Please visit www.plsclear.com to complete your request.

Unless otherwise noted, Scripture taken from the New American Standard Bible®, Copyright © 1960, 1962, 1963, 1968, 1971, 1972, 1973, 1975, 1977, 1995 by The Lockman Foundation. Used by permission.

Scripture quotations marked (ESV) are from The Holy Bible, English Standard Version® (ESV®), copyright © 2001 by Crossway, a publishing ministry of Good News Publishers. Used by permission. All rights reserved.

Scripture quotations marked (NIV) are taken from the Holy Bible, New International Version®, NIV®. Copyright © 1973, 1978, 1984, 2011 by Biblica, Inc.™ Used by permission of Zondervan.

British Library Cataloguing-in-Publication Data
A catalogue record for this book is available from the British Library

ISBN: 978-1-83973-224-9

Cover & Book Design: projectluz.com

Langham Partnership actively supports theological dialogue and an author's right to publish but does not necessarily endorse the views and opinions set forth here or in works referenced within this publication, nor can we guarantee technical and grammatical correctness. Langham Partnership does not accept any responsibility or liability to persons or property as a consequence of the reading, use or interpretation of its published content.

To my wife, Michal,
who is as responsible for this effort as I am.
She has sacrificed countless hours for this composition,
and her support has been unflagging and irreplaceable.

To my Lord, Jesus Christ.
Though I was once an enemy of the divine rule,
God's grace has transferred me from the dominion of darkness
into the kingdom of marvelous light.
Jesus alone is my refuge, my life, and my hope.

Contents

Acknowledgements xiii

Foreword xv

1   An Introduction to Demonological Studies 1

2   Demonology in a Globalized Age 11

3   The Criteria for a Demonology for the Global Church. 25

4   The Malevolent Activity of Demons 41

5   The Recorded Speech of Demons. 77

6   The Nature of Demons. 97

7   The Corporate Influence of Demons 109

8   The Purpose of a Demonology for the Global Church 121

9   The Challenges to a Demonology for the Global Church. 137

10 Demonology for the Global Church in the Days to Come. 151

Bibliography 157

Acknowledgements

I must first recognize Ramathate Dolamo, my doctoral supervisor with the University of South Africa. While this book is a distinct effort, his guidance in the construction of my doctoral work provided a solid foundation for this volume.

The assistance of Trevor Yoakum from *Ecole Supérieure Baptiste de Théologie de l'Afrique de l'Ouest (ESBTAO)* merits recognition. He offered invaluable corrections and contributions for the improvement of this work.

Finally, I wish to acknowledge the support of my fellow faculty members and the students at the Baptist Theological Seminary of Zambia. Many of the faculty have patiently guided me into a greater understanding of demonological issues in Africa. And the students never pass up an opportunity to test my demonology with stories and questions. I praise God for the grace of serving with you for his glory.

Foreword

I highly recommend this book.

Before I chose to read it, I wondered why a book on demonology needed to be written "for the global church." I had read many books on demonology and thought that as long as they were biblical, they would apply to all cultures and churches in any country of the world.

So far, so good.

But Scott has done careful study on how demons are regarded in different cultures, and he sheds light on how our cultures can shape our understanding of the demonic. Then he takes us to the Scripture, carefully building his theology by interpreting various relevant passages in their historical context and seeing their application to us. Culture can inform us, but it cannot lead he reminds us. If you are wondering, the answer is *yes*, this book actually lives up to its title!

Demonology for the Global Church avoids the sensationalism that is often evident in some books on demonology. Scott points out that there are many instances in Scripture where people were inhabited by demons. But this is not Satan's primary method of attacking the church. Demons work through temptations common to us all: moral impurity, lack of forgiveness, doctrinal heresies, and even politics! We do not have to "see demons" in order to realize they work behind the scenes, and we had better take Paul's admonition to "put on the full armor of God" (Eph 6:13 NIV).

Scott has done his homework. He quotes widely from various authors with different points of view and from different cultures, but he always directs us back to the Scriptures as the only reliable guide in our understanding of the unseen world. His aversion to sensationalism gives us the gift of perspective and balance. Discernment, he says, is always needed, but perhaps most needed when we can so easily go astray when we navigate the unseen world without sober reflection on the biblical data.

I was also intrigued by Scott's story. Brought up amid the forests of Canada, why did he end up in South Africa studying demonology? Looking back, we can see God's hand in it all; Scott needed a breadth of knowledge concerning other cultures to author a book that can be read by "the global church." Christians of all cultures will see that they have been heard, but then taken to the Bible as the only source of true understanding of a topic that is too often fraught with speculation and superstition.

This book would also be very appropriate for those who are skeptics, who either deny that demonic spirits exist or attribute their supposed reality to the overheated imaginations of religious fanatics. Scott's book is careful, sober, and grounded in scriptural exegesis and reflection. It is scholarly yet readable and applicable.

If you, like me, think you have read enough books on demonology and do not need to read another, give this book a careful reading. You will be informed, instructed, warned, and otherwise blessed.

Erwin W. Lutzer
Pastor Emeritus, The Moody Church, Chicago
Author of *God's Devil* and *Seven Snares of the Enemy*

1

An Introduction to Demonological Studies

Why Demonology?

Humanity does not have to venture far before encountering speculation and attestations of the demonic. Regardless of whether the global scientific and academic societies consider them credible, the reports of malevolent spiritual activity abound. The world burgeons with skepticism, curiosity, and obsession.

Consider the news. CNN alone has published a host of related news items. Previously in their photos section, Troi Anderson had publicly displayed photographs of the Maria Lionza cult in Venezuela, wherein spirits, both helpful and violent, reportedly inhabit many.[1] Journeying to Swaziland, Kyle Meyer depicted the casting out of demons in carefully framed black and white pictures.[2] Turn to CNN's videos and witness the apparent exorcisms of Bob Larson, complete with screaming and dramatic confrontations.[3] Watch the strange sights and sounds of various demonic encounters in a Pennsylvanian house, which even affected the film crew.[4] On the CNN website, read the article by Jake Simons on the Aymara people of Bolivia, which details the unusual religious blend used to counter misfortune and "harmful spirits."[5]

What about Kristine McGuire? She was featured in a piece by the Christian Broadcasting Network (CBN) as she proclaimed an unusual aversion toward

---

1. Troi Anderson, "Summoning Spirits in Venezuela," *CNN Photos* (16 January 2014).
2. Kyle Meyer, "Swaziland Church Battles Demons," *CNN Photos* (19 November 2013).
3. "Watch Pastor Perform Exorcisms," *CNN* (24 January 2014).
4. "Haunted House's 'Ghost' Attacks News Crew," *WPMT* (CNN Affiliate) (5 August 2014).
5. Jake Wallis Simons, "The 'Catholic Witchdoctors' of Bolivia: Where God and Ancient Spirits Collide," *CNN* (17 September 2014).

her past dealings with the occult.[6] She had boasted of being a self-identified "ghost hunter," but when she stumbled upon something demonic, something she deemed beyond her abilities, she cried out to Jesus for help.

Eowyn Stoddard speaks about "demonic bullying" in her piece circulated through the Gospel Coalition.[7] As a church planter, she sensed an evil presence and suffered through several unusual circumstances. Her concerns culminated as her toddler described horrific nightmares, which were incongruent with the knowledge and experiences of such a young child.[8] Even as Stoddard professes her continuing faith in the sovereign God of the Bible, she admits, "What we experienced was 'normal' for our context, and many other missionaries can testify to similar kinds of things." Based on biblical, communal, and personal data, she concluded that demons were involved.

Worse yet, brutal forms of ritualism, witchcraft, and occultism exist, and demonic and satanic forces elicit the credit. In April 2012, a so-called "baby factory" closed in southeastern Nigeria.[9] Police arrested three individuals for housing seven young women who were producing babies for sale. The purposes for trafficking children from such factories are numerous. In this instance, Oyekachi Orji, the assistant police superintendent, said, "The suspects usually lure young girls to get pregnant with a promise of 70,000 naira [$445] after having their babies, which they sell to ritualists." Even *News24* admitted in the article that "less commonly [babies purchased from these factories] are tortured and sacrificed in black magic rituals." Nigerian theologian Vincent Onyebuchi Nwankpa files such acts under witchcraft and comments, "There are many evidences in Nigeria of the atrocities that witches commit day after day, ranging from killing both born and unborn children, to deforming children in the womb and stopping the development of fetuses."[10] But how does all of

---

6. "Kristine McGuire: A Ghost Hunter Calls on Christ," *CBN TV and Video* (n.d.).

7. Eowyn Stoddard, "Dealing with Demons," *The Gospel Coalition* (9 December 2013).

8. Stoddard, "Dealing with Demons." Stoddard admits that people first assumed she was "imagining things" when blood was spilled on her door along with detecting an evil presence. But her skepticism quickly faded away, and her narrative insists that "the horrid climax was the nightmares that tormented our 2-year old son. For many months he'd wake up screaming . . . and we could not easily settle him back down. At two and a half, he was finally able to verbalize what he'd been dreaming about for the past few months. One of his most vivid dreams was about a woman with black hair and red eyes who wore only a bra and black pants and would offer him a basket of rotten fruit and force him to eat. His nightmare was X-rated, not a typical toddler-being-chased-by-a-bear dream."

9. "Nigeria Rescues Girls from 'Baby Factory,'" *News24* (13 April 2012).

10. Vincent Onyebuchi Nwankpa, *Understanding Cultural Perspectives, God's Word, and Missions: A Powerful Tool for Theologizing* (Bloomington, IN: Authorhouse, 2009), 99.

this relate to unseen evil entities? They regularly collect a portion of the blame, leading Nwankpa to conclude, "The evil power of Satan has not been removed from him [Satan]."[11]

We cannot avoid malevolent spirits in current events, and Christian history offers no respite for those who would wish to evade them. In his groundbreaking work, *Demonology of the Early Christian World*, Ferguson outlines the Jewish and Greek attitudes toward the demonic followed by the early Christian response to the phenomenon. Summarizing "generally held views" among Christian authors in the centuries after Christ and the apostles, Ferguson says:

> They accepted the reality of the spiritual world, in which there were both good angels and wicked demons. All were creatures of God and originally good. Some angels in the exercise of their free will, at some point, rebelled against God and fell from their heavenly abode. . . . The demons were responsible for the physical evils in the world, stood behind all false religion, induced the persecution of true religion, and tried to tempt men into sinning against God. Those [people] who did so were punished by serving the demons. The demons' spheres of activity, therefore, were the cosmos, governmental structures, and individuals. But on all levels their power was ultimately subject to God. Their defeat had been sealed and assured by the life, ministry, death, and resurrection of Jesus. . . . Meanwhile, those who believed in Jesus and followed the will of God had power over demons. This was dramatically demonstrated in the ability of Christians to drive away demons in the name of Jesus Christ. Wherever paganism was practiced and human beings gave themselves to the will of demons, there demonic influence was felt; but wherever the gospel was preached and the influence of Christ was felt, the demons were powerless.[12]

Just as the demonic confronts people in the present, so also people in the past have dealt with the topic's presence.

---

11. Nwankpa, *Understanding Cultural Perspectives*, 99.
12. Everett Ferguson, *Demonology of the Early Christian World* (New York: E. Mellen, 1984), 133–34.

Finally, the biblical pages scarcely stir without a reference to an evil supernatural being. A spirit afflicted King Saul.[13] The psalmist records that the Israelites sacrificed their children to demonic powers.[14] The Apocalypse of John even depicts a grand heavenly battle waged between Satan's host and the holy angels (Rev 12). The Synoptic Gospels and Acts are replete with examples of demonic activity. A serious scholar of Scripture must account for the demonic and grant the subject ample consideration.

Why demonology – the study of the demonic? We cannot help but engage it. Around the globe, throughout history, and across cultures, the topic demands both our attention and a Christian systematic theology due to the subject's inclusion in the Scriptures along with its persistent presence in our global age. On the one hand, devoid of necessary reflection on the doctrine of evil spirits, the Christian mind is misshapen, unable to produce a well-rounded response to the innumerable facets of the corporate and personal evils of the age. On the other hand, fueled by cultural perceptions and presumptions concerning the demonic, the Christian mind is bound, unable to mount a biblical defense against the schemes of the powers that plague every culture. May this work call the global church – both in the West and in the Majority World – back from her cultural, philosophical wanderings to embrace the demonology of the Bible.

Why Write on Demonology?

Bias, context, and perspective are always present and pertinent in any theological work. This book is no exception. Why would I, a child of rural eastern Canada, pursue such a topic as demonology in light of global considerations? When I was an undergraduate theological student at Moody Bible Institute in Chicago, a few of my professors introduced me to Christian theology abroad, particularly on the African continent. After encountering the seminal writings of the late

---

13. 1 Samuel 16:14 reads, "Now the Spirit of the LORD left Saul, and an evil spirit from the LORD terrified him." According to John Walton, Victor Matthews, and Mark Chavalas, "Just as the Spirit was able to give the positive attributes of courage, charisma, insight, wisdom and confidence, negative results could also be produced by spiritual influence. These would include fear, paranoia, indecisiveness, suspicion and shortsightedness." *IVP Bible Background Commentary: Old Testament* (Downers Grove, IL: InterVarsity, 2000), 306.

14. Psalm 106:37 says, "They even sacrificed their sons and their daughters to the demons." State Walton, Matthews, and Chavalas, "This word for demon is used elsewhere in the Old Testament only in Deut 32:17, but it is a well-known type of spirit/demon in Mesopotamia, where the term (shedu) describes a protective guardian mostly concerned with the individual's health and welfare. . . . A shedu could destroy one's health just as easily as it could protect it, so sacrifices to keep it placated were advisable. They were depicted as winged creatures." *IVP Bible Background Commentary: Old Testament*, 206.

John Mbiti, I read others like Kwame Bediako and Byang Kato. This background set the stage for my subsequent studies with Stellenbosch University and the University of South Africa.

Furthermore from 2010–17, I served in various capacities with an evangelical church in Chicago.[15] Though my responsibilities varied, I regularly found myself responding to Christians who recounted their confrontations with demonic spirits. Firsthand experiences also began to proliferate, and a thorough and biblical study of the subject was necessary since I desperately lacked knowledge and training in this area. Oddly enough, while American Bible schools openly resist the pressures of culture in some areas (e.g. sexual ethics), the American cultural tendency to downplay the demonic prevailed in my education up to that point.

Emerging from this purely practical genesis, I have continued to investigate the doctrines and debates in the demonological field. In 2017, I started serving at the Baptist Theological Seminary of Zambia in Lusaka, Zambia. The training process required a nine-month immersion into Zambian culture, language, and worldview. As members of a society exiting its pagan past and entering a "Christianized" era,[16] the experience of many of my Zambian brothers and sisters has loosely correlated with the witness of believers in the early church who also experienced struggles for freedom as they cast off the demons and gods of their ancestral religions. Because of their experience, I believe that the testimonies and leaders of newer Christian centers around the world are the most insightful as we frame the doctrine of demonology since they are often in tune with the subject through overt conflict with pernicious spiritual actors.

Yet experience should not equal theology. Relying on the biblical material is essential, especially as all cultures pollute Christian pneumatatology, the doctrine of the spirits, with deleterious attitudes of dismissiveness or excess.[17] While culture provides important context for how we exercise Christian virtues

---

15. Since "evangelicalism" is a word with many uses, clarification is in order. In this work it refers to, "The movement in modern Christianity, transcending denominational and confessional boundaries, that emphasizes conformity to the basic tenets of the faith and a missionary outreach of compassion and urgency. . . . Evangelicals regard Scripture as the divinely inspired record of God's revelation, the infallible, authoritative guide for faith and practice." R. V. Pierard, "Evangelicalism," in *Evangelical Dictionary of Theology*, ed. Walter A. Elwell (Grand Rapids: Baker Book House, 1984), 379.

16. Zambia publicly identifies itself as a "Christian nation."

17. Throughout this work, the general category of "pneumatatology" will be employed to encompass the theologizing of various kinds of spirits, including demons, angels, Satan, deceased ancestors, and other non-theistic beings. In that light, Satanology, demonology, angelology, and other classical fields will be folded together as subcategories under pneumatatology. However, demonology will be our narrower aim.

like hospitality, culture is no friend of demonology, regularly controlling and contorting the subject. Scripture is our theological loadstar, the light from above to guide our way. Let us now meditate upon the terms which will either power or shipwreck our journey.

What are some common terms to consider and clarify? A foray into demonological waters entails circumspect navigation, and one course-plotting tool is the definition of terms. If we do not clearly define the terms involved in the voyage, we are liable to confusion and error. Especially in demonology, conceptions concerning particular words are only constant in their variance, and thus we must outline the intended meaning of the terms which will feature in this work.

Spirits

The flexibility of this word in modern usage is astounding. From its prominent role in the term *zeitgeist* to its association with pleasant feelings, the word has a plethora of diversity.[18] Even within the Scriptures, a number of meanings persist, but in the Old Testament (e.g. 1 Kgs 22:22) and the New Testament (e.g. Acts 23:9), the original words translated as "spirit" can refer to nonhuman and nondivine persons of varying levels of moral quality. In the Old Testament, the word "spirit" reflects the Hebrew word *ruach*, a flexible term that means "spirit, wind, or breath."[19]

A similar flexibility is in the Greek word *pneuma*, and one of the primary meanings of the word is "an independent noncorporeal being, in contrast to a being that can be perceived by the physical senses."[20] Concerning New Testament usage, "*Pneuma* was also a term for noncorporeal, conscious, malevolent beings. . . . Spirits were not considered invariably malevolent; some are 'of God' which makes it necessary to distinguish between spirits."[21] The Bible routinely clarifies with an adjective of some kind, whether it be for example an "unclean" spirit as in Mark 1:23 or a "ministering" spirit as in Hebrews 1:14.

---

18. *Zeitgeist* is commonly translated from German into English as "spirit of the age." Also sometimes it is said, "They were in high spirits," referring to people being jovial.

19. Warren Baker and Eugene Carpenter. "רוּחַ" in *The Complete Word Study Dictionary: Old Testament* (Chattanooga, TN: AMG, 2003), 1040.

20. "πνεῦμα," Frederick W. Danker, Walter Bauer, William F. Arndt, and F. Wilbur Gingrich, *Greek-English Lexicon of the New Testament and Other Early Christian Literature*, 3rd ed. (Chicago: University of Chicago Press, 2000), 833.

21. J. W. Simpson, Jr. "Spirit," in *The International Standard Bible Encyclopedia* (Grand Rapids: Eerdmans, 1979), *PC Study Bible Database*.

By virtue of our material, we will predominantly wield the word "spirit" in a supernatural sense pertaining to demonic powers.

Angels

In general, we will attempt to retain the biblical usage of angel from the Old and New Testaments. The *Dictionary of Deities and Demons in the Bible* provides a pair of helpful definitions. Concerning the Hebrew word *malak*, "The Bible characteristically uses *malāk* to designate a human messenger (e.g. 1 Sam 11:4; 1 Kgs 19:2). A smaller number of the over 200 occurrences of the word in the Old Testament refer to God's supernatural emissaries."[22] The biblical Greek equivalent *angelos* receives a similar treatment. "*Angelos* . . . is in Greek, Early Jewish and Christian literature the most common designation of an otherworldly being who mediates between God and humans. . . . It is sometimes used of human messengers."[23] From the Scriptures, angel can refer to either human or supernatural messengers, but for the purpose of this study, supernatural actors will be the common referent of this umbrella term, which covers both malevolent and elect agents.[24]

Sons of God

In the Old Testament, the phrase "sons of God" (*bene elohim*) usually corresponds to the general meaning of angel, fallen or exalted. While the New Testament has a concept of "sons of God" which primarily relates to redeemed humanity (e.g. 1 John 3:1), this early terminology of the "sons of God" refers to those beings who were directly created by God – heavenly beings (e.g. Job 1:6).[25] Carol Newsom comments, "Although no single term corresponding precisely to the English word 'angels' occurs in the Hebrew Bible, there is a rich vocabulary for such beings. Some of the expressions either denote their divine status . . . 'sons of God' . . . 'gods' . . . or denote their special sanctity . . . 'holy

---

22. S. A. Meier, "Angel I," in *Dictionary of Deities and Demons in the Bible*, ed. K. Van Der Toorn, Bob Becking, and Pieter Willem Van Der Horst (Leiden: Brill, 1999), 46.

23. J. W. Van Henten, "Angel II," *Dictionary of Deities and Demons*, 50.

24. Spirit and angel are nearly parallel terms under these stated definitions.

25. In the New Testament, one pertinent exception is found in Luke 3:38, the genealogy of Jesus, where Adam is designated the "son of God." In this text, Adam is a son of God by virtue of creation, not redemption.

ones.'... Other terms denote their functions."[26] The same group is in mind when we speak of angels and the sons of God, and the terms portray various aspects of that group's identity. We need not call them "divine" as Newsom does, but we can affirm their unique creation relationship with God, even as we acknowledge that they cannot be ontological rivals or equals with the supreme Being – the Creator of the spirits.

Demons

Joanne Kuemmerlin-McLean rightfully states the difficulty of studying the demonic in the Old Testament, "it does not seem that there is a single term in biblical Hebrew which can consistently and unquestionably be translated as 'demon.'"[27] In *Demons: What the Bible Really Says about the Powers of Darkness*, Michael Heiser extensively details the Old Testament's numerous words for demon-like entities. He argues that "the New Testament has fewer words for the powers of darkness and loses some of the nuanced presentation of evil spirits found in the Old Testament."[28] Most of the cohesive concept of demons comes from a canonical viewing of the Old Testament, and the role of the Septuagint is significant in that process since it first translated the Old Testament Hebrew terms into Greek.

When we read an English Bible, demons rarely feature in the Old Testament texts, and "spirit" is the prevalent name for demon-like beings. The word "demon" appears in Deuteronomy 32:17 and Psalm 106:37. The related term "satyr" or "goat demon" is used in Leviticus 17:7 and 2 Chronicles 11:15. However, these few references do not mean that the demonic powers are nearly nonexistent in the Old Testament, and we will see how the Old Testament employs other terms like "sons of God," "spirits," and "gods" (*elohim*) to portray beings in the supernatural realm.

The term "demon" originates from the Greek *daimon/daimonion*, and thus the New Testament is replete with easily identifiable references to demons.[29] In Greek circles, *daimon/daimonion* had some variance in meaning. Ancient

---

26. Carol A. Newsom, "Angels," in *The Anchor Bible Dictionary*, ed. D. N. Freedman, vol. 1 (New York: Doubleday, 1992), 248.

27. Joanne K. Kuemmerlin-McLean, "Demons," in *The Anchor Bible Dictionary*, ed. D. N. Freedman, vol. 2 (New York, NY: Doubleday, 1992), 138.

28. Michael S. Heiser, *Demons: What the Bible Really Says about the Powers of Darkness* (Bellingham, WA: Lexham, 2020), 2.

29. "There are over one hundred references to demons in the Bible, most of them occurring in the New Testament." C. Fred Dickason, *Angels: Elect and Evil* (Chicago: Moody, 1975), 151.

Greek literature used the term for "powerful entities that transcend ordinary experience," including what they called gods, as well as evil spirits.[30] But by the time and context of the apostolic writings, C. Fred Dickason asserts, "The final stage of its usage is found in the New Testament, where all demons are evil and work as Satan's agents."[31] One exception to that rule is found in Acts 17:18, where Athenian philosophers presume that Paul is advocating for foreign gods.[32] The Athenians did not use the word with an evil or negative connotation. In this work, we will use the word "demon" to refer to corrupt supernatural spirits, in keeping with the predominant biblical concept. No good or amoral demons exist. Spirits, angels, sons of God, demons – with these few terms in hand, we can traverse the road ahead and encounter more along the way.

Where Are We Going?

In this introductory chapter, we have outlined the information necessary to undertake this mission into biblical demonology.[33] First, we exposed the relevance of the matter so we might understand that the topic is not a temporary or trite issue. Throughout the world, history, and Scripture, we encounter demonology. Second, we discussed the background and context of this author, elucidating the biases that will invariably appear in this effort. Third, four terms required definition, as they appear regularly throughout this argumentation.

What lies ahead? We cannot approach demonology without recognizing that the world has entered a globalized age, and this reality requires that we grant additional attention to culture and multicultural concerns, since our cultures significantly shape our perception of the demonic. We will also outline criteria by which we can wisely navigate our study of Christian demonology.

---

30. "δαιμόνιον," Danker, Bauer, Arndt, and Gingrich, *Greek-English Lexicon*, 210.

31. Dickason, *Angels: Elect and Evil*, 153.

32. One commentator portrays the situation with an intriguing question. "In this scene Luke seeks not to provide detailed information about legal proceedings, but to create a mood. Is Luke playing on a misunderstanding, attributing to the audience an interpretation of the word 'anastasis' as a name for a goddess rather than a word meaning resurrection (RSV)? (Chrysostom understood the text this way.) The plural [*daimonia*], 'divinities,' certainly does not prove this." Hans Conzelmann, *Acts of the Apostles: A Commentary on the Acts of the Apostles*, Hermeneia (Minneapolis: Fortress, 1987), 139.

33. In this work, I will regularly refer to "biblical demonology." This phrase exposes the difference between cultural demonologies and biblical demonology in a manner similar to Merrill Unger's use of the term in his book *Biblical Demonology*. The use of biblical demonology does not imply that this work is inherently a biblical theology of the demonic, as this book falls under systematic theology and not biblical theology in relation to theological genre.

These criteria will guide us through the activity of demonic beings, along with their biblical speeches, ontology, and corporate influence. With a firm grip on the substance of the doctrine, we will draw out the purpose of demonology in Christian theology and ministry. Finally, we will address the challenges against demonology in our times, like skepticism and sensationalism, before pondering the importance of demonology in the global church in the days ahead. Let us embark on this journey together!

2

Demonology in a Globalized Age

We, God's church around the world, have a problem. Regardless of where we reside, whether in Asia, Europe, South America, Africa, or elsewhere, we tend to express a view of the demonic that is more in line with our culture than our Bible. This is understandable since our childhood ideas concerning the demonic formed within our cultural backgrounds. But ignoring this problem is a recipe for chaos and conflict in our local churches. We must acknowledge the depth of the relationship between our cultures and our perceptions of the demonic. Only once we perceive those connections can the Scriptures transform our demonology.

The Relationship of Demonology and Culture

How aware are we of our own cultural frameworks? The urban African, the rural American, the seaside Asian, and every variety of human beings on the earth have one thought about culture in common: we all appreciate our own ways of life, treasuring them even as we are occasionally annoyed by aspects of our own culture. While we usually operate unconsciously under the parameters of culture, we ought to ask and unveil what should be obvious.

What is culture itself? Kato summarizes, "Culture is the whole system of living made up of what a society knows and does."[1] Kevin Vanhoozer posits a similar definition: "'Culture' refers to the beliefs, values, and practices that characterize human life together at a particular place and time."[2] Kathryn

---

1. Byang Kato, *African Cultural Revolution and The Christian Faith* (Jos, Nigeria: Challenge, 1976), 7.

2. Kevin J. Vanhoozer, *The Drama of Doctrine* (Louisville: Westminster John Knox, 2005), 129.

Tanner broadens the matter even further. Arguing that every culture contains disagreeing parties under its umbrella, she states:

> [Culture] forms the basis for conflict as it forms the basis for shared beliefs and sentiments. Whether or not culture is a common focus of agreement, culture binds people together as a common focus for engagement. The struggle over culture, whether and to whatever extent it produces true commonality of beliefs or sentiments, presumes culture as common stakes: all parties at least agree on the importance of the cultural items that they struggle to define and connect up with one another.[3]

While these complexities deserve acknowledgement, our study will emphasize the unity of cultures, in contrast to each culture's internal incongruencies. Thus when speaking about cultural differences, the subject at hand is inter-diversity not intra-diversity.

Virtually every culture has a category for unseen spirits and demonic beings. Dismissing the anti-supernatural assumptions of modern Western thought, Keith Ferdinando argues:

> Most peoples, for most of history, have believed in spirits, witchcraft, and sorcery. The Ohio State University research project found that some 74% of 488 societies studied throughout the world had possession beliefs, including 81% of 11 African societies studied. . . . While truth is not established by majorities, the great consensus of most of humanity through time suggests that it may be modern skepticism which is idiosyncratic, and that the burden of proof should fall upon those who deny the reality of such phenomena.[4]

Humanity perceives spirits as a reality, even in a supposedly enlightened (Westernized) age. Indeed, "belief in spirits is widespread in the ancient and modern world."[5] This acceptance of malignant supernatural beings places the burden on those who discount the possibility of their existence. Similar to the

---

3. Kathryn Tanner, *Theories of Culture: A New Agenda for Theology* (Minneapolis: Fortress, 1997), 57.

4. Keith Ferdinando, *The Triumph of Christ in African Perspective: A Study of Demonology and Redemption in the African Context* (Carlisle, UK: Paternoster, 1999), 376.

5. Gordon Stein, *The Encyclopedia of the Paranormal* (Amherst, NY: Prometheus, 1996), 713.

challenge of defending atheism, the ability to martial sufficient evidence to prove the nonexistence of demons is what should rightly arouse skepticism.

This nearly universal perspective surfaces in our cultures. Whether in Kato's Jaba culture that believes in *Kuno* (a Satan-like figure) or in another culture that squeamishly avoids a so-called "haunted house," our cultural worldviews ground our viewpoints concerning the spiritual realm. But it seems that some minds have a greater attunement to this subject. For example, the Akan people in Africa attest to one peculiar type of spiritual being. Kwame Bediako depicts these fiends:

> Mmoatia are supposed to be mysterious creatures with superhuman powers, that dwell deep in the forest; they are believed to be tiny, with feet that point backwards; suspending themselves from trees, they wait for an unwary hunter in the pitch darkness of the night. At their head, as their spirit, is Sasabonsam with bloodshot eyes. His name has found its way in Akan Christian vocabulary to designate the devil.[6]

And so the Christians of that area sing, "*Sasabonsom* the evil spirit has troubled hunters for many years."[7]

In general, Africans have no qualms admitting the reality of evil spirits. Concerning the issues of evil, witchcraft, and spirits, Gerrit Brand comments that "a certain family resemblance" exists among the African peoples and "even those who deny the existence of an absolutely evil spirit, would not deny that spirits sometimes do evil."[8] Brand concludes, "In that sense, they all recognize the existence of invisible 'forces of evil.'"[9]

But Africa does not have exclusive rights to the subject, for we can look eastward. Asian cultures also acknowledge the spirits. John Livingstone Nevius was a missionary to China, arriving in 1854. As he commenced his language and culture studies, he confessed his skepticism. "I brought with me to China a strong conviction that a belief in demons, and communications with spiritual beings, belongs exclusively to a barbarous and superstitious age, and at present can consist only with mental weakness and want of culture."[10] At this early juncture, Nevius was a child of his culture, assuming that all

---

6. Kwame Bediako, *Jesus and the Gospel in Africa* (New York: Orbis, 2004), 10.
7. Bediako, *Jesus and the Gospel in Africa*, 10.
8. Gerrit Brand, *Speaking of a Fabulous Ghost* (Frankfurt Am Main: P. Lang, 2002), 96.
9. Brand, *Speaking of a Fabulous Ghost*, 96.
10. John Livingstone Nevius, *Demon Possession and Allied Themes* (Memphis, TN: General Books, 1894), 4.

others were lacking. He even tried to convince his teacher of his "ignorance and imagination."[11] Yet as Nevius listened, he "could not but notice, however, the striking resemblance between some of his (teacher's) statements of alleged facts and the demonology of Scripture."[12] He then began diligent research to document cases and locations of demonological phenomena during his ministry. The Chinese knew the spirits. The Bible displayed the truth about them. And Nevius eventually yielded his skepticism.

More recently, Samuel Hio-Kee Ooi testified concerning his experience in Malaysia:

> I moved to Kota Kinabalu, Sabah to teach in a seminary more than two years ago. This city is filled with a mixture of indigenous people groups, including Kadazam, Dozon, Murut, etc, and Chinese, as well as Muslim Malay. That many of the indigenous groups are Christians does not mean a total discard of their traditional animistic worldviews and practices. Chinese popular religious practices are common and different gods are worshipped in Kota Kinabalu as in other Chinese communities. Spirit possessions are frequently heard of. And during Chinese New Year season this year, one of my students had a "battle" with the spirit of Guanyin . . . a Bodhisava contextualized in Chinese Buddhism, who possessed her elder sister's body.[13]

Ooi, who speaks from a Chinese perspective, dwells in a multicultural area of Malaysia. He depicts that diverse neighborhood as keenly aware of the spiritual forces that are at work. He actually laments that Christianity's presence is often Westernized, which often "dismisses" what he calls the "world of spirits," and therefore the embrace of Christianity is half-hearted.[14]

Concerning the West, we need only to scratch the thin veneer of European culture's naturalism to reveal its ancient acknowledgement of the demonic powers. In addition to Europe's historic forms of paganism and spiritism, works like *The Malleus Maleficarum* (The Hammer of Witches) demonstrate Europe's underlying commitment to the reality of the spiritual realm, demonic power, and occult practices. The first question of the volume literally poses the possibility that the denial of witches who cooperate with demons could

---

11. Nevius, *Demon Possession*, 4.
12. Nevius, 4.
13. Samuel Hio-Kee Ooi, "A Study of Strategic Level Spiritual Warfare from a Chinese Perspective," *Asian Journal of Pentecostal Studies* 9, no. 1 (2006), 143.
14. Ooi, "Study of Strategic Level Spiritual Warfare," 144.

amount to heresy![15] The answer to this question is astonishing in its certainty: "Any man who gravely errs in an exposition of Holy Scripture is rightly considered to be a heretic. And whosoever thinks otherwise concerning these matters [witches and demons] which touch the faith that the Holy Roman Church holds is a heretic. There is the Faith."[16]

Ultimately, spirits are a recognized reality in the cultures of the world, demanding a Christian response that a biblical demonology offers. If nearly every culture has inherent information concerning demonology (or pneumatatology), this fact certainly affects our Christian theology and practice. For not only do a majority of cultures mention spirits and demons, but the word of God has revealed the true activities and identities of these spirits. We would be callous to ignore (or despiritualize and demythologize) the Scriptures and say little as the world waits for Christianity's answer concerning these cultural and experiential norms. We also would be foolish to authoritatively supplant or supplement the Scripture's perspective of the demonic with ancient or modern cultural information and affirm what the Bible does not, potentially serving as a conduit for demonic deceptions.

The Problems and Opportunities of Globalization

The global church has another problem. Not only are our ideas about demons largely derived from our cultural backgrounds, but all of our cultural demonologies increasingly collide in our churches. The globe that we once knew has changed. We inhabit a world in transition, and the church has transformed with it. For better or for worse, the forces of globalization appear to be unstoppable, though they may occasionally slow due to regional or global events. Economic and cultural structures are extending beyond their historical and traditional regions. Robert Schreiter details that in recent decades, one parish in north Chicago encompassed "fifty-three language groups . . . five of which held services" in a single church each week.[17] Cultures are intersecting, and they even mingle in educational, economic, and ecclesiological contexts. With such diversity in our communities, what issue would present an obvious arena for disagreement? Demonology! How can we prevent such conflict?

---

15. Montague Summers, trans., *The Malleus Maleficarum of Heinrich Kramer and James Sprenger* (1928, reprint Downers Grove, IL: Dover, 1971), 33.

16. Summers, *Malleus Maleficarum*, 33

17. Robert J. Schreiter, "Multicultural Ministry: Theory, Practice, Theology," *New Theology Review* 5, no. 3 (1992).

Sarojini Nadar, a South African theologian, criticizes globalization as a front for Western colonial interests. She considers it a means to further Western ideals and systems.[18] Inspired by the Nigerian author Justin Ukpong, Nadar advocates for a better way. Instead of settling for a Western globalization, she requests that we form a global village. "In Africa, the term 'village' implies community and mutuality, both of which – at the very least – include the notions of respect, justice and equity."[19] In other words, our rich cultural diversity compels us to eschew all forms of cultural supremacy in favor of a global village.

Our pursuit of this type of church village sounds almost like a search for heaven on earth. It is a heart-warming sentiment, but is it not a touch utopian for the harsh realities of our age? The ability to completely avoid cultural clashes in the church under Christ's banner is seemingly absent from the New Testament, and a multicultural age of peace fails to crystalize until the final chapters of Revelation.[20] Yet shall we not seek such harmony now, especially as we approach demonology? Perhaps the potential problems that globalization provokes could also be opportunities?

---

18. Sarojini Nadar, "Contextual Theological Education in Africa," *The Ecumenical Review* 59, no. 2-3 (2007), 235–41.

19. Nadar, "Contextual Theological Education in Africa," 236.

20. Even in missions, Christianity has often arrived with baggage that is detrimental to culture. Especially as we intersect and interact with the theology of those who are experiencing pronounced cultural change from the introduction of Christianity into their area, we should reaffirm some concerns. For instance, Kato, who converted from traditional religion to Christianity, hears and understands the cries of many around the world who lament that "missionaries have destroyed our culture." Byang Kato, *Theological Pitfalls in Africa* (Kisumu, Kenya: Evangel, 1975), 174. Spoiling the noble effort of proclaiming the gospel, some people forced or misled recipients of the good news into completely abandoning their pre-Christian culture. Entire cultures have been irreparably altered in ways more in keeping with Western culture than biblical imperative. Yet Kato correctly points us to the iconoclastic God-fearing Ephesians in Acts 19. Kato, *Theological Pitfalls in Africa*, 174.

When false religion is completely integrated into the culture and history of a people, the transformative power of the gospel will naturally enact societal change, even in the absence of any unjust actions of cultural colonialism. As Mbiti says, "In traditional society, there are no irreligious people. . . . A person cannot detach himself from the religion of his group, for to do so is to be severed from his roots, his foundation, his context of security, his kinships and the entire group of those who make him aware of his own existence." John Mbiti, *African Religions and Philosophy* (Portsmouth, NH: Heinemann, 1990), 2. In that light, Kato uncomfortably asserts,

> If religion is what gives direction to life, Christianity must necessarily change the life-style or culture of the African. . . . Is it worth preserving the 'juju' if the converted Christian will be tempted to go back to 'Egypt' or 'the house of Laban?' Where lies the unique claim of Christ which is supposed to supersede even kin relationships (Matt. 12:46–50)? Should national pride or cultural heritage come before Christ? New Testament Christianity has a strong negative answer to that. 'I count all things to be loss in view of the surpassing value of knowing Christ Jesus my Lord, for whom I have suffered the loss of all things, and count them but rubbish in order that I may gain Christ' (Phil. 3:8).

The Christian must think critically concerning how to speak in this cultural milieu. Scott Moreau calls for a dynamic and comprehensive contextualization, intonating that the difficulty increases in an urban, globalized context. He says:

> Contextualization, like local societies, should never be thought of as static. At the very least, each generation of Christians in a culture will need to contextualize the Christian faith in ways that are faithful to Scripture and indigenous to them. In times of radical cultural change (urbanization, acculturation, globalization) the process of contextualizing the faith will be a never-ending one, offering rich opportunity for the people of God to be rethinking and living out their faith in light of ways Scripture challenges them and their societies as they change.[21]

Thankfully, Moreau's words remind us of the joy of this challenge, as the shifting culture provides us another opportunity to return to the word of God, instigating meditation and renewing communication. There is our opportunity! Globalization has left our Christian communities with the opportunity to learn from one another and find Scripture as our common ground, especially in contentious issues like demonology.

Demonology for Multicultural Communities

In many lands, we can no longer train, minister, and theologize with a single culture in mind. A monolithic, uninfluenced culture, untouched by other forces, is increasingly becoming a norm of the past. Urbanization, drawing people from rural areas to city communities, has created a great intersection of cultures in centers throughout the world. Consider Dubai, where foreigners compose about 80 percent of the city's population of 2.7 million![22] Globalization, with the expanding ease of travel and foreign commerce, has led to cultural cross-pollination on an unparalleled scale. Thus in many contexts, we must speak about multicultural society. While not directly speaking to the emergence of multicultural communities, Timothy Tennent recognizes the pressing need, saying:

Kato, *Theological Pitfalls in Africa*, 175. In America, Africa, Asia, and the world, our allegiance to Christianity should trump any affection to our past way of life. The Christian convert discovers a new foundation and a new existence, and a Christian community has a new relationship to its culture and history, redefined by the arbiter – biblical revelation.

21. A. Scott Moreau, "Contextualization That Is Comprehensive," *Missiology: An International Review* 34, no. 3 (2006), 326.

22. Geoffrey Migiro, "The Most Diverse Cities in the World," *WorldAtlas*, 28 March 2019.

In the past, such global exposure and intentional cross-cultural preparation was generally afforded only to those preparing for the missions field, and that often took place in separate degree programs. Today, all of our academic and vocational preparation must train with a deeper sensitivity to the larger global context in which Christian ministry takes place. Christianity has always been a faith for the world. Therefore, even students preparing to pastor white, clapboard churches in the plains of the Midwest or in rural hills of Georgia cannot escape the forces of globalization and religious pluralism they will meet there.[23]

What is true for theology as a whole is proper for the subdiscipline of demonology. Are we prepared to present a biblical demonology that is simultaneously accessible to our culturally diverse hearers?

Throughout this work, we will recognize the challenges and opportunities of multicultural communities. However, we should not misconstrue the word "multicultural" with "multiculturalism." According to Sarah Song, "The term 'multicultural' is often used as a descriptive term to characterize the fact of diversity in a society," but the supporters of multiculturalism often prescribe particular social, political policies to address that diversity.[24] Our primary aim is to describe the phenomenon in contrast with monocultural societies. In other words, we will not venture into sociological debates concerning multiculturalism. Rather, the demonology we discuss will exhibit an awareness of multicultural and monocultural contexts.

As we consider how to best address the subject of demonology in the multicultural context, complexity again intensifies. Communication and cohesiveness can break down if one culture asserts its information above so-called lesser cultures, often slandered and alienated by labels like "primitive," "rural," and "traditional" that assume the superiority of "modern," "urban," and "progressive." Multicultural community, in the "global village in a local village" sense, cannot survive in this context, and a certain party's values will inherently dominate, dictate, or structure the diverse whole.

We should expect disagreement, and Moreau encourages us to view contextualization as "a two-way process in which all sides contribute."[25] That is, no culture should attempt to gain in the process. Whether in a traditional

---

23. Timothy C. Tennent, *Theology in the Context of World Christianity* (Grand Rapids: Zondervan, 2007), 19.

24. Sarah Song, "Multiculturalism," *The Stanford Encyclopedia of Philosophy*, Spring 2017 Edition.

25. Moreau, "Contextualization," 327.

missionary context (i.e. one culture entering another) or in a multicultural community (i.e. many cultures forming one society), we should not aim "to show the members of the second culture how they should express their faith and their lives" based on our cultural affinities.[26] A multicultural Christian community, for example a church, parachurch group, or theological seminary, requires everyone involved to be culturally sensitive, socially adept, and intentionally reflective to stem the imposition of their own cultural presuppositions concerning the demonic.

The difficulty of this contextualization endeavor in multicultural society is further complicated by the complexity of culture itself.[27] Kraft distinguishes between "surface-level culture" and "deep-level culture."[28] Surface-level culture pertains to behavior and practices, and deep-level culture relates to thinking and value commitments – one's worldview, which includes conclusions concerning the existence and relevance of spirits. A multicultural Christian community can (and should) graciously embrace many forms of learned surface-level culture, creating an elegant tapestry of unity and diversity among God's people. But the peril rests in how to respond to diverse worldviews – deep-level culture. We should respect different ways of thinking, for example about parenting methods, but Christ calls his followers to deny themselves, to repent, and to be renewed in their thinking. As Christians, our culturally conditioned worldviews are not static. We learn from one another under the leadership of the Spirit and the word, growing into an interconnected body. In a multicultural community, this growth leads to an increasingly shared worldview through biblical instruction, even as we still encounter and enjoy the diversity of our cultures.

The dangers at this point are many. As we approach the subject of demonology, we do not desire the outright destruction of anyone's worldview, since culture (both familial and societal) contains elements of God's creative wisdom. Of course, this argument does not mean a retention of old religious practices. Religious systems are not merely cultural systems. Rather, we are wise to recall that supernatural powers work through false religions. If we uncritically seek a "sympathetic perspective" of cultural/religious pasts while

---

26. Moreau, 327.

27. The complexity intensifies even as we consider the regional worldviews (e.g. European, African), because within these broader categories, diversity flourishes, though "there may be similarities here and there." John S. Pobee, *Toward an African Theology* (Nashville: Abingdon, 1979), 44.

28. Charles H. Kraft, "Culture, Worldview and Contextualization," in *Perspectives on the World Christian Movement* (Pasadena: William Carey, 1998), 385.

claiming Christianity, we should expect to encounter allegiance problems in the supernatural realm.[29] The ease with which cultures can simultaneously adopt conflicting religious systems is astonishing. Therefore, the project is to treasure culture even as we weed out the religious allegiances that are rooted in our cultures rather than Christ.

Preconversion worldviews (deep-level culture) cannot be entirely retained, lest we relegate Christ, not taking him along "in grave movements – of sickness and death, of plague and suffering in general."[30] Crises encourage reversion to "traditional and well-tried methods of countering the effects of evil and giving assurance in a world of uncertainty and danger."[31] Our ingrained cultural commitments concerning demonology often erupt from deep caverns of the self in such difficult predicaments.

In the pitfalls and harvests of weeding and cultivating culture as Christians, the multicultural community blossoms into hope. When we are united together in this culture-retaining, self-crucifying, Christ-glorifying expedition, we find in one another the courage to proceed. As we pursue Christ, the body buoys us by those who both yield elements of their own cultures and retain culture that is good and compatible with the faith. And our cultural demonologies, which operate in our worldview (deep-level culture), cannot stay the same.

As we approach the subject of the demonic, the theological project, which inherently involves contextualizing God's truth into cultural categories, must account for the complicating factor of cultural diversity in our communities. How should pastors frame Christian doctrine when people of numerous cultures fill the pews? How should evangelists declare Christ to the masses when the Asian, the African, and the European are all within their oratorical reach? How should theologians craft their papers on demonology when their readers are no longer culturally homogeneous? Walter Hollenweger, while outlining intercultural theology, offers an answer, "The point of contact between our traditions and the new theologies from the [Majority World] is Scripture."[32] How can we bridge the evangelistic, theological, and pastoral gaps in multicultural communities and contexts? We start and finish with fidelity to the word of God, granting it supremacy over us and our cultural backgrounds.

---

29. Bediako, *Jesus and the Gospel in Africa*, 71. To be fair, Bediako is not recklessly seeking that perspective, but his argumentation certainly opens the door for a view on African religious past which could lead to syncretism.

30. Kwesi Dickson, "African Theology: Origin, Methodology and Content," *The Journal of Religious Thought* 32, no. 2 (1975): 36.

31. Dickson, "African Theology," 36.

32. Walter Hollenweger, "Intercultural Theology," *Theology Today* 43, no. 1 (1986): 29.

Possessing divine credentials, Scripture alone has the right to rebuke and rule over every culture, preserving what is good and excising what is not.[33] Any other form of social unity in the church is like a cultural imperialism, the dictating of values from one culture to another. Scripture supplies the only sure and perfect grounds for Christian commonality, unity within diversity, and clarity concerning the demonic.

The Dead Ends for Addressing Demonology in Multicultural Communities

Demonology could enter the multicultural sphere and splinter the community. Let us avoid some dead ends. First, the most tempting way to create harmony is by declaring that every culture is right. This affirming and seemingly friendly route promises peace, but it fails to deliver any meaningful sense of concord. For when a spiritual or demonic crisis arises, the cacophony of equally "truthful" (yet somehow divergent) voices delivers no help or clarity. One cultural participant may claim that a demonized person requires exorcism, and then another will prescribe a conflicting remedy. Meanwhile, a Westerner is urging calm since a spirit could not possibly inhabit the person! Who is right? "Everyone" is an appallingly unprofitable and nonsensical response. Affirming everyone's point of view would simply undermine any sense of reality or truth whatsoever. If we advocate for this avenue in demonology and other areas, only a truth-less hopelessness will bond the community.

Second, the most ignorant dead end is to issue a moratorium on dialogue concerning the realm of pneumatatology. Realizing that the diverse opinions on the issue could result in something other than an open and cohesive village, one could potentially seek silence as a remedy. Demonology would be relegated to family discussion or personal musings, but ecclesiological and public discourse concerning spirits would be taboo. Unfortunately, this scenario is the experience of many of our Majority World brothers and sisters who journey to the West. An entire realm of their life is unaddressed by the church, even if they join an ethnically diverse congregation. Silence falls short of providing authentic harmony and cohesion. Demonology would be but one among many arenas of disagreement in a multicultural Christian community. Widespread

---

33. According to Kato, "We must accept both the positive and negative aspects of all cultures." Byang Kato, "Contextualization of the Gospel: Theological Perspective," [Typescript] in *Byang H. Kato: 1936–1975: Perspectives of an African Theologian: The Writings of Byang H. Kato Th.D.*, ACTEA Data CD, 1.

isolation and disintegration would be a presumable outcome. Demonology would be, at least, a social force for division rather than union.

Third, the most oppressive response would be for people in a "power culture" within the multicultural community to assert their ideas on the whole, manufacturing a forced harmony.[34] This possible response would not reflect the broader group. Yet per Nadar's concern about globalization, this phenomenon is what we are currently experiencing. Globalization is expanding the influence of Western values, for example anti-supernaturalism, largely at the expense of the ideals of other cultures.[35] Of course, people in different cultures can learn from one another. But strengths and weaknesses are difficult to discern when the observer is culturally conditioned and self-serving (consciously or unconsciously). The imposing influence of Western scientific naturalism has certainly had a negative effect on the other cultural approaches to perceiving and articulating the demonic. Even many Christians are hesitant to share about their experiences in multiethnic company, fearing that all who hold beliefs in the spirits are prejudged as backward. However, to attain a harmonious, cohesive, multicultural Christian community, one cultural party (Western or otherwise) cannot insist upon their own ethnic understanding – to the exclusion or diminution of others.

Having rejected these dead ends, the only plausible way forward in addressing demonology in a multicultural context is for a thorough and voluntary agreement of the cultural parties. On what essentials do they need to agree? They must acknowledge that no culture, including their own, is completely or predominantly correct. After recognizing human fallibility, then the stage is set for divine revelation, Creator to creatures, which corrects, instructs, and unites the multicultural village. Only God can utter infallibly concerning reality since God is truth, while every culture offers but a finite, incomplete understanding of reality. Our finite selves, even in solidarity with others to form a distinct community, do not determine reality; we only express our fallible perception of it. For reality to be known, the infinite God

---

34. By using the term "power culture," we are acknowledging that within any multicultural community, certain groups have advantages. For example, the church could be historically associated with one group's area culture. People of one culture may have greater access to or control of financial resources. Or the primary language of worship in the congregation could be the first language of one group. Seemingly unavoidable realities like these in our multicultural age can position some as members of power cultures.

35. Even the format of this book, prepared according to standards which have arisen from largely Western influences, demonstrates the predominance of Western culture in the global education and literary spheres.

must speak, declaring truth from lie – which he voiced in the Bible and in the incarnation of Jesus Christ.[36]

But in elevating Scripture to unite the multicultural village, are we merely homogenizing our diversity? No! Scripture becomes our touchstone for discussion and disagreement even as we contextualize in our various cultural backgrounds. And the alternative to elevating Scripture is untenable. Apart from God's truth, the truth which can authoritatively enter cultural diversity, people in multicultural settings will find themselves trapped within a conscious or subconscious struggle for cultural supremacy. But the word of God can set us free, urging us forward in hope, challenging every culture, and forging a unity among people of every cultural background in Christ.

True multicultural harmony is found in biblical supremacy. In the midst of diversity, Scripture is the meeting place. It is the only suitable arbiter in disagreement and the only sure guide in crisis. Demonology elicits plenty of disagreements and crises! But God's word beckons all of us, despite our divided backgrounds and conflicting thoughts, to bond in the words that transcend us. This divine Truth, who supersedes our immanent cultural "realities," is the only solution for unity about demonology in a multicultural context.

The Unmasking of Cultural Demonology

Our global age, replete with multicultural communities of endless varieties, tests the quality of our theological acumen. If our doctrine on the demonic cannot speak outside a single culture, wilting under the heat of multicultural demands, our formulations are merely the exposition of culture rather than the proper exegesis of Scripture. Our diverse times have unmasked cultural demonology; the moniker of "Christian" no longer cloaks it.

As we consider cultural demonology, let us first differentiate between cultural application and cultural theology. Cultural application is a discipline and art which attempts to translate and contextualize truth into a culture. This contextualization is valuable and needed, though fraught with danger and confusion in a multicultural scenario. It assumes the biblical worldview but tries to convey it into cultural terms without altering or corrupting the

---

36. See John 14:6. Ernst Haenchen, Robert W. Funk, and Ulrich Busse state, "It is the conviction of the Evangelist that no one has ever seen the Father: he is simply inaccessible in his transcendence. But it is precisely in this context that the mission and significance of Jesus becomes visible: he is the 'way,' to the Father, and as such the 'truth' and the 'life,' disclosing the divine truth." Ernst Haenchen, Robert W. Funk, and Ulrich Busse, *John: A Commentary on the Gospel of John*, Hermeneia (Philadelphia: Fortress, 1984), 125.

original message. Cultural theology, as defined in this work, pertains to the imposition of cultural priorities and ideas upon the biblical worldview. This practice redefines the original intentions of the holy text in both insignificant and monumental ways, pitting culture and exegesis against one another as sparring partners in the definition of reality and truth.

Cultural theology is frail at best. It not only is bound by culture but also by time, since every culture is constantly in flux. A culture-bound theology demonstrates the emptiness of its truth claims by dissolving in time, lacking the substance of an external divine authority, or by floundering outside its culture, since the diverse Christian community does not respect it as a reflection of biblical truth. The multicultural context demonstrates that we need more than a cultural theology; we need a theology of the demonic from Scripture that can speak in every culture, even as it transforms the cultures it enters.

We are interacting with the norms of the age – globalization and multicultural societies. As the world shrinks through business, immigration, and opportunity, the formation of communities such as churches, seminaries, and other organizations increasingly challenges Christianity to reflect the diversity of its adherents. But how will we take up the task of teaching and theologizing amidst the people of many cultures who inhabit such spaces? By what paradigm must we approach demonology?

To address these questions properly, we have detailed the connection between culture and pneumatatology, with most cultures perceiving the reality of the spirits. Majority World thought (past and present) is particularly attuned to these spiritual concepts. We have prescribed theological sensitivity to this reality, since the Scriptures themselves affirm a worldview that includes such beings.

But what about those instances in which people of many cultures coexist in Christian spaces? This rapidly increasing social phenomenon further heightens the need for Christians to affirm the biblical contents. We should not champion one cultural perspective at the expense of the others. Since Scripture, by the Spirit of God, unites God's people from every background, a demonology that exhibits multicultural awareness must emphasize the Scripture.

We are not able to present a view of the demonic that is entirely free of cultural bias or perfectly adept in the diversity of the age, but we need not be beholden to culture's rule. Let us pursue theological reflection that both rebukes and affirms aspects of all cultural backgrounds through the exegesis, proclamation, and exaltation of God's discourse concerning the demonic.

3

The Criteria for a Demonology for the Global Church

The Sabbath day in Capernaum probably began as usual. The inhabitants of northern Galilee populated the synagogue, and a reading of the Torah commenced. But the authoritative ministry of a new teacher, Jesus, astonished the crowd. A man "with an unclean spirit" screamed, interrupting the religious proceedings with vitriol. "What have you to do with us, Jesus of Nazareth? Have you come to destroy us? I know who you are – the Holy One of God" (Mark 1:21–24 ESV).[1] Mark reports this scene early in his gospel concerning the Christ, and the reader is curious. What just happened? What is an unclean spirit, or a demon, since Mark uses those terms interchangeably?[2]

Any thoughtful student of the Scriptures experiences questions or wonder after beholding the spectacle of these spiritual confrontations. This passage in Mark is only the beginning, for Job, Zechariah, Luke, Ephesians, Revelation, and other biblical books also elicit queries concerning supernatural beings of a despicable quality. Beings of the demonic realm are not peripheral and inconsequential; they are prominent opponents of the divine Protagonist of the redemption narrative.

The biblical inclusion of exorcisms and other demonic encounters are not without purpose. In the case of Mark 1, the writer selects a demon to supply an initial testimony concerning the Messiah. Robert Guelich explains the demonic

---

1. According to Robert Guelich, "The demon addresses Jesus as 'Jesus, the Nazarene.' After asking about the purpose of Jesus' coming, the spirit then demonstrates his knowledge of Jesus' true identity, 'The Holy One of God.'" Robert A. Guelich, *Mark 1–8:26* (Grand Rapids: Zondervan, 1989), 57.

2. Guelich states, "'The unclean spirits' . . . represents a common Jewish designation for demons. . . . The two expressions appear synonymously in Mark (3:30 cf. 3:22; 7:25 cf. 7:26, 29, 30)." Guelich, *Mark 1–8:26*, 56.

outburst saying, "This announcement shows the demon's awareness of who Jesus is and that Jesus is His superior.... In so doing he identifies Jesus for Mark's audience or reader."[3] We cannot gloss over what is essential to the Scripture's proclamation.

Yet questions about the demonic not only flow from sacred text, they well up from the pages of daily life and the cultural volumes that flood our world. How should we understand the demonic in the Bible? By what framework should we categorize the spiritual phenomena that occur in our homes, our churches, and our nations?

Any theological examination demands criteria. Why? It would be easy for someone to blurt out pages of words strung together, and when reaching the end, we could uncritically declare, "That sounds good to me." But personal approval is not a suitable standard for discerning the truth of a theological work! Consider this basic example: some people are born liking a particular food, yet they change their mind concerning it throughout their lifetime. How then could we expect fleeting approval to judge accurately and concretely concerning truth, specifically concerning the demonic?

Too often, we can fall prey to poor criteria. What are some measures that we should avoid? While certainly not an exhaustive list, here are three. First, linked to the false end of personal approval, we must reject communal approval as a false criterion for demonological study. Consensus cannot and does not determine what is right and true. Conventional wisdom of cultures and communities often sways and shifts with the winds of time. Popular opinion is not the criterion for reliability.

Second, pragmatism is an unsuitable criterion for our treatment of demonology. While the attitude of "do whatever works" bombards us, the practical outworking of a dogma does not properly verify the doctrine itself. Orthodoxy should guide orthopraxy, not vice versa.

Third, reason alone should not guide our demonology. Theology should be reasonable, but it is not purely reason. Rather, reason, or naturalistic logic, should serve divine revelation, and this arrangement may result in seemingly unreasonable, non-naturalistic conclusions, for example affirming the virgin birth. A naturalistic standard or criterion for the examination of the demonic, a decidedly non-naturalistic field, would impose an intellectual handicap. But since these are poor criteria, what then shall we employ for the pages ahead?

---

3. Guelich, 57.

Biblical Centrality

The revelation of God through the Old and New Testaments must be the first and primary standard for assessing the reliability of the following study on demonology.[4] The Bible presents divine words concerning reality, and it frames the world as we should understand it. How can physical manuscripts and ancient codices represent in human language the mind and authority of the incomprehensible? The Holy Writ claims to have divine origins, and it beckons to our minds and hearts – our very lives – with an irrepressible call for worship, obedience, and glory to its Creator. But how can this be? The Bible can be the word of God because God was and is the Word (John 1:1, 14). By this allusion to Johannine doctrine, the present case is that the character of the incarnation of the second person of the Trinity demonstrates how the message and mission of the divine can be rightly imaged from the incomprehensible to the finitely accessible. As the Son took on flesh via the hypostatic union without the denial or degradation of his eternal, unchangeable nature, the words of God have been revealed without error in their assertions, free from any betrayal of God's intention and reputation. As the Son condescended to our estate, uniting with our nature, speaking our words, relating to our weakness, the Scriptures have sufficiently communicated to us on our level concerning what God would have us know, cherish, and follow.

The revelation of Christ proclaims that God can be met, and the written revelation declares that God can be heard. Furthermore, in both cases, God exerts authority over us. The incarnate Word was considered peculiar during his earthly dispensation, for he acted as one who had authority, in contrast to other teachers (Luke 4:32). The written word also bears divine authority, repeatedly claiming, "Thus says the Lord," relaying the message of Christ, and insisting on the inspiration of other authors. The Scriptures and the average book on the shelf do not share the same weighty authoritative language.

The Bible alone avoids the excesses and dismissals of competing cultural positions concerning the demonic. Can Scripture claim supremacy over the norms of the world's cultures? Absolutely. The word of God rebukes cultural corruption even as it upholds societal strengths. God, by virtue of his creator authority, can interject into the patterns of human community, whether by theophany or sacred writings. Only the Supreme Being is qualified to rule creation, and while humanity vainly attempts to manipulate, create, rule, or

---

4. As this author is an evangelical Protestant, additional resources such as the Apocrypha are respected as historical works, but they are not elevated to the status of divine revelation alongside the sixty-six canonical books of the Old and New Testaments.

transform culture in some lasting sense, only God has the moral credentials to speak into culture without deserving question and skepticism. God and God's word can authoritatively proclaim who we are, what we are supposed to do and think, and why we exist. The Scriptures transcend our cultural norms and cultural demonologies, inherently influencing every contextual opinion that conflicts with revelation.[5] Merrill Unger argues:

> In no sphere is this fidelity to reality and verity more advantageously displayed than in the domain dealing with demonological phenomena, wherein distortion and extravagance are elsewhere so notoriously rampant. Whether it be a matter of the revelation of basic demonological truth, or the appraisal of varied demonological phenomena, or the complex description of a people under the paralyzing power of evil supernaturalism, the Bible's unerring criteria are absolutely trustworthy. The character of Biblical demonology itself, as clear and unerringly recorded truth, qualifies it as a wholly reliable standard of evaluation in appraising the character of demonology in general.[6]

Unger, along with the word of God itself, reminds us that the Scriptures alone are the suitable starting place for demonological thought.

Why is divine revelation so reliable and necessary for the project of demonology? Let us outline three strengths which set apart the Bible as essential for theologizing concerning the demonic. First the Scriptures, which are "breathed out by God," claim to speak for the Creator.[7] The triune God of

---

5. However, the ways in which Christian minds translate and apply the divine message into various cultures is worthy of careful critique. Hermeneutically speaking, this means that we should diligently monitor our use of Scripture. We are not without presuppositions which "have been formed by historical, social, and cultural processes." Dirk J. Smit, "Reading the Bible and the [Un]official Interpretive Culture," *Neotestamentica* 28, no. 2 (1994): 309. Dangers abound, and if we fail to contextualize biblical imperatives properly, we can inadvertently (or intentionally and sinisterly) weaponize Christianity into an instrument of cultural destruction, usually to our own cultural and egotistical advantage.

6. Merrill F. Unger, *Biblical Demonology* (Wheaton, IL: Scripture, 1952), 21.

7. While a complete defense of the perfection and divine nature of Scripture is not the purpose of our efforts, it merits a brief comment. Paul refers to "all Scripture" as being "breathed out by God" in 2 Tim 3:16 ESV, and his word choice is pregnant with meaning. Lea and Griffin explain, "The idea the term presents is that God has breathed his character into Scripture so that it is inherently inspired. Paul was not asserting that the Scriptures are inspiring in that they breathe information about God into us, even though the statement is true. The Scriptures owe their origin and distinctiveness to God himself. This is the abiding character of Scripture." Thomas D. Lea and Hayne P. Griffin Jr, *1, 2 Timothy, Titus*, New American Commentary (Nashville: B & H, 1992), 236.

the Bible does not merely claim divinity; revelation attests that he, through Jesus Christ, is the Creator of all things. A number of texts could be cited, but John 1:3 is direct: "All things came into being through Him [the Word, Jesus Christ], and apart from Him not even one thing came into being that has come into being" (ESV).[8] Everything that exists was created by the biblical God. This verse and its phrasing, especially with the inclusion of the word "nothing," "emphasizes the involvement of the Logos in the bringing into being all of reality except the uncreated reality of God."[9] But why does God's identity as Creator matter?

The owner of a car might be able to testify concerning the vehicle's qualities. But surely, if we wish to apprehend the fullness of the car's purpose and abilities, we should consult the maker, the designer, or the creator of the vehicle. At least, we would consult a technical manual provided by the manufacturer. In a similar fashion, the Creator of all that exists is the authority on reality. While observing creation may be helpful, shall we not prioritize consulting the Creator, who imbued the world and its inhabitants with purpose and life? We must seek Jesus and his revelation to us concerning the demonic.

Did God create the demonic realm? Although Psalm 148:1–6 mentions the Lord's decree to create the angels, the biblical text never says, "God created demons."[10] Yet from the Johannine gospel, we assert that nothing exists apart from his original creative work. Because demons are inherently a part of creation, or more precisely the corruption thereof, the Creator's perspective on reality, revealed through the Scriptures, is paramount.[11]

Second, if we accept the biblical literature as truthful, demons are finite, supernatural spirits who operate differently than humans. Although humans are spiritual beings, we are also corporeal. This ontological distinction is a

---

8. According to R. C. H. Lenski, "'All things came into being' since the beginning, the Logos through whom they were called into being existed before the beginning, from eternity. . . . The Son is from all eternity 'the uncreated Word.'" R. C. H. Lenski, *The Interpretation of St. John's Gospel* (Minneapolis: Augsburg, 1961), 36–37.

9. Gerald L. Borchert, *John 1–11*, New American Commentary (Nashville: B & H, 2002), 107. This sets us against Bultmann's interpretation of this verse and in agreement with Haenchen, Funk, and Busse's critique of Bultmann's error (Bultmann claimed that the Logos was only responsible for the "world of men.") (Haenchen, Funk, and Busse, *John*, 109–113).

10. Robert G. Bratcher and William D. Reyburn state, "The psalmist calls upon all heavenly creatures to praise Yahweh. . . . These verses [verse 5–6] give the reason for the command to praise Yahweh: all things and beings in the realms above were created by his command, and so they are his creatures, his servants." Robert G. Bratcher and William D. Reyburn, *A Handbook on Psalms*, UBS Old Testament Handbook Series (New York: United Bible Societies, 1993), PC Study Bible Database.

11. As Creator and Sustainer of all, the Lord's perspective *is* reality.

problem! As an illustration may we suppose that a fish, which has never been anything except a fish, wished to think critically about the experience of a bird breathing oxygen. This fish could hardly expect to ascertain a proper analysis from its uninformed perspective. Yes, some similarities exist since the fish processes oxygen via its gills, but would not the fish's study fall inadequately short if it failed to rest upon the counsel of a being that breathes oxygen in an analogous manner to a bird? In keeping with the fictitious nature of this illustration, perhaps the fish could even consult a bird directly.

To analyze the subject of spirits critically, we require communication with a supernatural spirit. Who among the spirits should we believe? The infinite Spirit, the Creator God should be our first recourse, and the divine being prohibits all forms of occult inquiry. Through Scripture, God speaks about what seems alien to us. A supernatural subject – the demonic – requires a supernatural explanation.

Third and hand in hand with the earlier two points, human beings are flawed and morally compromised evaluators. Without reproof and accountability, we regularly think in a manner that inflates and advances our self-importance. The temptation to let this attitude seep into our demonology is strong because we prefer to proffer a vision of the demonic that is manageable and easily comprehensible. Human sentiment, pride, and pragmatism can all interfere.

Instead, Scripture scrapes away the intellectual debris which clutters our consideration of the demonic. Biblical clarity cures our simplicities and extravagancies and instructs us concerning the divine outlook which confounds our evaluative expectations. Shunning a bold self-reliance on our weak human intuition and intellectual capacity, we turn to the God of all truth, knowledge, and wisdom. The Bible's message concerning the demonic must be the primary criterion for our work.

Hermeneutical Consistency

If we wish to grant Scripture the primary role in our demonology, we must then ask, which interpretation of Scripture?[12] Consider how hosts of men and

---

12. Any substantial study of Scripture requires an open declaration of the underlying hermeneutical assumptions. And a dearth of reflection invariably births selfish or skewed interpretations. What is hermeneutics? Snodgrass says, "Hermeneutics is the process by which texts are understood and appropriated." Klyne R. Snodgrass, "Introduction to a Hermeneutics of Identity," *Bibliotheca Sacra* 168 (Jan–Mar, 2011): 3. When we use this process, we aim to recognize and focus the lenses through which we observe and comprehend a particular work, in this case the Bible. This endeavor inevitably guides us to the giant question which always surfaces, what does the Bible mean?

women in the New Testament encountered Jesus of Nazareth and left with various impressions and interpretations of his role and identity. Mark records the following:

> Jesus went out, along with His disciples, to the villages of Caesarea Philippi; and on the way He questioned His disciples, saying to them, "Who do people say that I am?" They told Him, saying, "John the Baptist; and others say Elijah; and others, one of the prophets." And He continued questioning them: "But who do you say that I am?" Peter answered and said to Him, "You are the Christ." (Mark 8:27–29)[13]

If the exact representation of God's nature in human flesh, the Messiah who had come to bless the nations of the earth, could be misunderstood and misinterpreted, should we not expect the revealed words of God – the Bible – to spark a variety of positions and opinions? Thus the annals of history are replete with competing ideas concerning the divine library of sixty-six books. The demonic has garnered the same diversity of opinions, and debate in this realm has provoked the composition of comparative works such as *Understanding Spiritual Warfare: Four Views*.[14]

But how do we recognize sound interpretation of texts about the demonic in Scripture? Hermeneutical standards are essential for evaluating any claim concerning biblical revelation. In addition to our earlier comments, let us propose a few necessary hermeneutical guidelines that pertain to demonology so that this teaching on the demonic may be consistent with the Scriptures.[15]

First, in developing a hermeneutical consistency that reflects the biblical material, progressive revelation cultivates needed perspective in interpretation.

---

13. Craig Evans states, "God himself had declared Jesus to be his Son ([Mark] 1:11; cf. 9:7), with the demonic world chiming in with fearful acknowledgement (1:24; 3:11; 5:7). But now Jesus is interested in knowing human opinion, that of the general public and then that of his own disciples." Craig A. Evans, *Mark 8:27–16:20* (Nashville: Thomas Nelson, 2001), 14.

14. Walter Wink, David Powlison, Gregory Boyd, C. Peter Wagner, and Rebecca Greenwood, *Understanding Spiritual Warfare: Four Views*, ed. James K. Beilby and Paul R. Eddy (Grand Rapids: Baker Academic, 2012).

15. While the desire to be thoroughly biblical is commendable, we must acknowledge that all Scripture interpretation is through a lens composed of our own faith, reason, culture, and tradition by which we encounter the revelation of God in his word. Christian theology must account for these realities, embracing the divine gifts of logic and culture even as they are reformed and revised by the Scriptures themselves. We lean upon reason, knowing that we will be found unreasonable. We rely on the historical contributions to the faith, daring to let the Scriptures refresh ancient doctrinal formulations. We embrace hermeneutical methods, prepared for the very object we study to reinterpret us. Our philosophy must constantly and completely submit to the word of God.

The human composers and compilers of the Bible did not complete their volumes in a single night. While the New Testament documents arose in a short timeframe, the formation of the Old Testament was a substantial process. At least it seems so from a finite, chronological perspective. Wayne Grudem says, "This collection of absolutely authoritative words from God grew in size throughout the time of Israel's history."[16] The content of the Bible gradually increased, and the redemptive plot of the overarching narrative, along with the worldview it espoused, advanced.

As even the triune nature of God is not immediately or fully expounded by the early volumes of Scripture, we should not anticipate divine revelation to articulate a complete treatment of the demonic in the first book of the canon. Heiser says, "the vocabulary for evil spirits in the Old Testament appears to have no unifying principle."[17] That idea should not surprise us, since many other doctrines also awaited the definition and clarity that would arrive later in history. Thus, as revelation slowly accumulated, it progressively disclosed the identity of Satan and the demonic, especially through the surprising entrance of the incarnate Christ and his earthly ministry. With the Messiah's coming, interactions that once occurred in heavenly places (Job 1–2) began to occur on earth (Matt 4). The Bible reflects this escalation, from the cryptic serpent in the garden to the unmasked dragon in the third heaven, "the serpent of old who is called the devil and Satan" (Rev 12:9).[18] While biblical harmony exists concerning the demonic, the text provides progressive clarity instead of strict continuity because of the nature of unfolding revelation.

Second, another hermeneutical point that demands consistency concerns the original intention of the text. Any passage can elicit a torrent of meanings from two similar people, and the divide can be even greater when age, culture, and training backgrounds differ. Thus who or what dictates meaning? Since the Scriptures self-attest to be from God through the superintended authorship of men and the divine perspective is more valuable than ours, we should not

---

16. Wayne Grudem, *Systematic Theology: An Introduction to Biblical Doctrine* (Grand Rapids: Zondervan, 2000), 55.

17. Michael S. Heiser, *Demons: What the Bible Really Says about the Powers of Darkness* (Bellingham, WA: Lexham, 2020), 8.

18. Robert G. Bratcher and Howard A. Hatton state, "That ancient serpent: this is a reference to the Devil as the snake in the Garden of Eden." Robert G. Bratcher and Howard A. Hatton, *A Handbook on the Revelation to John*, UBS New Testament Handbook Series (New York: United Bible Societies, 1993), *PC Study Bible Database*.

choose to dictate the meaning.[19] God owns the meaning. As Kevin Vanhoozer asserts, "the author, as the one who originates and guarantees authenticity, also commands and controls meanings. Authorship implies ownership."[20] Imposed meanings gain us little, for "Divine authority does not attach to whatever meaning other people may attach to the words."[21] Rather as lowly beings under an omniscient, omnipotent, eternal, infinite Spirit, humility is demanded of us. Similar to the Lord unfurling a whirlwind retort to Job's impetuousness (Job 38:1–11), the Bible, by virtue of God's nature, insists that we receive and accept its meaning.[22]

While many Christians freely hold opinions on a range of biblical topics, including demonology, these opinions do not and should not override the authorial intentions of the biblical texts. Sadly, perplexing ideas concerning the demonic have cropped up that have little affinity with what the Bible originally intended to convey. In history, the books of Jubilees and 1 Enoch are examples of how, hundreds of years after the original events, interpretations of Scripture can evolve and add to what the inspired canon communicates. While still helpful in discovering ancient Jewish demonology, such books also wander into the genre of historical fiction. Because these works are not in the canon, we cannot embrace their extrabiblical retelling of history with confidence.

Consider a more recent example. Karl Barth offers a peculiar doctrine on the demonic. He argues that demons are an uncreated byproduct of God's creative work! Barth says:

> What is the origin and nature of the devil and demons? The only possible answer is that their origin and nature lie in nothingness.... As we cannot deny the peculiar existence of

---

19. Let us mimic the attitude of the psalmist who cried, "Make me know Your ways, LORD; Teach me Your paths. Lead me in Your truth and teach me, For You are the God of my salvation; For You I wait all the day" (Ps 25:4–5).

20. Kevin J. Vanhoozer, *Is There a Meaning in This Text?* (Grand Rapids: Zondervan, 1998), 46.

21. Vern Poythress, "Divine Meaning of Scripture," *Westminster Theological Journal* 48 (1986): 250.

22. Robert Alden states,
> God was not asking for information but reminding his challenger [Job] that the divine will had not been represented by what he said. We all speak 'words without knowledge' unless they are the properly understood and interpreted words of the Bible. Since they had such limited revelation and were immersed in a pool of similarly benighted others, it is amazing that Job and the others spoke as much truth as they did. Nevertheless, as will become clear, all missed the mark and spoke out of their darkness.

Robert L. Alden, *Job* (Nashville: B & H, 1993), 369.

nothingness, we cannot deny their existence. They are null and void, but they are not nothing. . . . God has not created them, and therefore they are not creaturely. . . . They are nothingness in its dynamic, to the extent that it has form and power and movement and activity. This is how Holy Scripture understands this alien element.[23]

A brief reading of Barth's vision of the demonic reveals that his assessment does not match the tone and tenor of the biblical narrative. Lest our treatment of Barth be labeled as a disrespectful outlier, Geoffrey Bromiley specifically mentions Barth's weakness in this realm with the following warning: "Unfortunately [Barth] does not back up the objection with any direct biblical material. . . . Yet he . . . lays himself open to criticism at a vital point: Is he really obeying scripture as the criterion of dogmatic purity and truth?"[24] Even though Barth claims the authority of the Bible and wields it effectively on many subjects, we must question on this point if he understands the intention of the biblical authors, for the concept of nothingness appears to be wholly extrabiblical.[25] Therefore, we should be critical and self-reflective in order to weed out philosophies and personal opinions. But how should we discern authorial intent?

Third, to discover the original intent of the authors, further biblical studies on the subject should breathe interpretive wisdom into any issues which arise.[26]

---

23. Karl Barth, *Church Dogmatics*, vol. 3 (Peabody, MA: Hendrickson, 2010), 523.

24. Geoffrey W. Bromiley, *Introduction to the Theology of Karl Barth* (Grand Rapids: Eerdmans, 1979), 155.

25. For a lengthy discussion of Karl Barth's demonology, please see Scott D. MacDonald, "Personal or Impersonal? An Analysis of Karl Barth and Merrill Unger's Perspectives on the Personhood of the Demonic" (MTh Thesis: Stellenbosch University, 2013).

26. While our current perspectives and agendas are diverse and fluid, the original authors' background, style, and objectives are set and often self-evident within their writings. But we cannot enter the human authors' minds, nor are we the original recipients of their books! Poythress considers this roadblock: "They did not write with us directly in view. Nor did they foresee all our circumstances and needs. We can still overhear what they said to people in their own time, but that is not the same as hearing them speak to us. How do we know what they want us to do with their words, if they did not have us in mind?" Poythress, "Divine Meaning of Scripture," 244.

What can we do? Are we trapped in the torturous position of perceiving divine revelation but never truly receiving it? No. Instead, we must take refuge in the divine intentions and the significance those words have for us today. We should apply Scripture with the original context in mind, ever asking, "What applications of a biblical passage does God approve?" (Poythress, 248). Yet at the same time, we confess by faith that only the Spirit of God can help us do this task properly. And while we do not suspend the counsel of reason and experience, the Spirit and faith are necessary for seeking meaning from a divine text. As Vanhoozer states, "To believe that there is meaning in texts is . . . an act of faith." Vanhoozer, *Is There a Meaning*, 30–31.

The context of Scripture is crucial, especially that of the story or chapter, book, and human author. Thankfully, since we understand the entire Bible to have a single divine Composer, we can obtain guidance from every book. Roy Zuck highlights the importance of context with an example:

> Understanding a word or sentence in its context is another aspect of normal interpretation, of how we normally and usually approach any written material. A single work or even a sentence may have several meanings depending on the context in which it is used. The word trunk may mean a part of a tree, the proboscis of an elephant, a compartment at the rear of a car, a piece of luggage.... Obviously it cannot mean all these things or even several of them at once in a single usage. The reader can determine its meaning based on how it is used in the sentence.[27]

Of course, confusion between a tree and a piece of luggage is usually more humorous than perilous. But when we are dealing with the word of God, confusion does not elicit laughter, particularly as we consider demonology.

Let us hear the human authors of the Bible concerning their intended message on demonology by virtue of the One who superintended their authorship. Peter testifies, "But know this first of all, that no prophecy of Scripture becomes a matter of someone's own interpretation, for no prophecy was ever made by an act of human will, but men moved by the Holy Spirit spoke from God" (2 Pet 1:20–21).[28] As we study these hallowed texts concerning not-so-holy spirits, let us approach them with Poythress' refrain, "What matters is

---

27. Roy B. Zuck, *Basic Bible Interpretation* (Wheaton, IL: Victor, 1991), 65.
28. According to Thomas Schreiner,
> Peter likely was attacking the opponents, arguing that they interpreted prophesy to support their own views. In doing so they resisted the proper interpretation given by the apostles.... Peter's argument, then, is that the readers must pay attention to the prophetic word as it is interpreted by the apostles, for the Old Testament prophesies are not a matter of personal interpretation but have been authoritatively interpreted by the apostles....
> The meaning of [2 Pet 1] v. 20, then, is that the interpretation by the apostles does not come from them but ultimately has a divine source, for prophecy comes from God.... By definition prophecy is a divine work and cannot be attributed to the ingenuity or native gifts of human beings....
> We have strong biblical support here for what B. B. Warfield called concursus. Both human beings and God were fully involved in the process of inspiration.... Concursus means that both God and human beings contributed to the prophetic word. Ultimately, however, and most significantly, these human words are God's words.... Peter, of course, referred only to the prophets here, but by extension we are justified in concluding that what Peter said about the prophets is also true of the New Testament canon. These writers also spoke from God and were carried

what God means. To find this out, we must interpret the words in accordance with what we know about God."[29] According to who he is and what he says, God is our authority in this demonological study, via the meaning and intention of his word. May our interpretations take "place in subjection to God's authority, control, and presence."[30]

What is a spirit? What is a demon? Lest we impose our human conceptualizations upon the text, we must take refuge in the biblical text when such questions arise, supported (not led) by other contextual considerations such as ancient Near Eastern culture and historical interpretations.

Historical Faithfulness

The theological task is not a recent development. Throughout the history and locations of Christianity, godly minds have studied demonology for millennia. Apart from explicit biblical testimony, we should journey circumspectly so as not to deviate from theological agreement across history.

Why should we grant such a position to human thoughts of times past? On our pursuit of demonology, these thoughts safeguard us from invention. If we attempt to develop an interpretation of Scripture that is unprecedented in the history of the church – or if heretics alone champion it – we should proceed with caution! Surely if the Spirit of God was active among Christians in ages past, should we not avoid the arrogant assertion that we have finally discovered a grand but hidden truth? Rather, the contributions of the saints should guide us in proper and biblical paths, away from the treachery of theological invention. Yes, they were human and prone to error as we are, but we should sidestep a conflict with the preponderance of church history unless biblically prescribed.

For instance, why should we rush to conflict with the great thinkers of the Christian church concerning the demonic? Surely what they said about the spiritual powers is not without wisdom and value! Augustine pleading in *The City of God against the Pagans* should be a guide to us. He says, "Do not desire false and deceitful gods. Abjure these: despise them, and spring forth into true

---

along by the Holy Spirit. Evangelical theology rightly infers from this that the Scriptures are authoritative, infallible, and inerrant, for God's words must be true.

Thomas R. Schreiner, *1, 2 Peter, Jude*, New American Commentary (Nashville: B & H, 2003), 322–23.

29. Poythress, "Divine Meaning of Scripture," 250.

30. Vern Poythress, "Christ the Only Savior of Interpretation," *Westminster Theological Journal* 50, no. 2 (1988): 306.

liberty. They are not gods; they are malignant spirits, to whom your eternal felicity is a punishment. . . . If you desire to approach the Blessed City, then, shun the fellowship of demons."[31] The preponderance of historical Christian doctrine openly instructs on such demonic powers and their influences, and we should be slow to deviate from them.

Historical interpretations can provide insight concerning our study of demonology. What other old guides can we recruit for our modern expedition? We should include the prominent confessions of the church. Although we could present many, let us grant attention to a couple of key historical statements that relate to demonology. However, we must keep in mind that in short summations of Christian doctrine, demons are not usually a primary feature. The Nicene Creed asserts, "I believe in one God, the Father Almighty, Maker of heaven and earth, and *of all things visible and invisible.*"[32] In article twenty the Augsburg Confession states, "For man's powers without the Holy Ghost are full of ungodly affections, and are too weak to do works which are good in God's sight. Besides, *they are in the power of the devil who impels men to divers sins, to ungodly opinions, to open crimes.*"[33] Finally, the Westminster Larger Catechism declares:

> How did God create angels? God created all the angels spirits, immortal, holy, excelling in knowledge, mighty in power, to execute his commandments, and to praise his name, yet subject to change. . . .
>
> What is God's providence toward angels? *God by his providence permitted some of the angels, willfully and irrecoverably, to fall into sin and damnation, limiting and ordering that, and all their sins, to his own glory*; and established the rest in holiness and happiness; employing them all, at his pleasure, in the administrations of his power, mercy, and justice.[34]

While these excerpts from historical documents uncover many issues which merit further consideration, we will let the Scriptures unveil those

---

31. Augustine, *The City of God against the Pagans*, ed. R. W. Dyson (Cambridge: Cambridge University Press, 2002), 92–93.
32. "The Nicene Creed Circa 381 A.D.," *A Puritan's Mind*. Emphasis added.
33. "The Augsburg Confession – by Philip Melancthon (1497–1560)," *A Puritan's Mind*. Emphasis added.
34. "Westminster Larger Catechism," Questions 16 and 19, *A Puritan's Mind*. Emphasis supplied.

themes in their proper time and place. In the meantime, we have accomplished our point: We should seek historical faithfulness to avoid interpretive hazards.

Theological Harmony

The final stated criterion for this expedition into demonology is theological harmony. While the phrase sounds agreeable, we could easily misinterpret it. What does theological harmony mean, and what does it require?

To begin, let us outline what the criterion of theological harmony does not entail. To avoid confusion and false standards, here are two faulty understandings of theological harmony. First, we could assume that we must necessarily agree with other points of view, even those from outside of historical orthodoxy. But while we could hypothetically seek such a goal, we could certainly not blend and unite every viewpoint, and most critically, we would scar the biblical worldview beyond recognition due to the innumerable incisions and amputations required to suit so many opinions. Harmony cannot exist apart from the rejection of false teaching.[35]

Second, in our aim to avoid misunderstanding concerning theological harmony, theology is not always under obligation to produce harmonious thoughts and dispositions. Whether the subject is death, sin, or demons, we should not expect that theology continually stimulates harmony when the topics at hand are sinister or alarming. Of course, Christians have hope and victory through salvation, but a glance into the darkness can aptly produce a shiver.

Having addressed what theological harmony does not mean, how then will it appropriately function as a criterion in our demonology? Initially, we should ensure that the entire endeavor is in tune with our theological formulations. Every conclusion must be in place, properly structured to convey a sense of harmony within the field of demonology. While it would seem oddly fitting for a study of the demonic to be beset with chaos and disjunction, internal consistency should aid one's judgment of this work's quality.

Furthermore, the interdependence of this argumentation of demonology should stand as self-evident. As each section relates to others, the overall content should interrelate. The work stands and falls as a coherent whole founded upon the word of God. Lord willing, the parts should fit together rather than being unrelated sections.

---

35. Theological harmony concerning the demonic can only resound once the cacophonous cloud of claptrap surrounding the subject is swept away.

The purpose for this criterion is two-fold. First, order, while not synonymous with a strong argument, does support the power of an argument by ushering one toward illumination and away from confusion. Second, a systematically interwoven demonology that reflects and defends the word of God is less likely to attract criticism concerning its method. Rather, skepticism and opposition pass along to the source of the study itself – the Scriptures. Perhaps those who would oppose this work would not aim at the messenger but at the Message. Hope upon hope to those who bristle at this project, please forgive the frailties of the messenger and yield to the Message of Scripture in entirety. For the Bible paints our foes and allies in the world across the canvas of redemptive history. Accept these criteria of biblical centrality, hermeneutical consistency, historical faithfulness, and theological harmony as we begin to examine the content of the doctrine itself.

4

The Malevolent Activity of Demons

Have you never felt uncomfortable reflecting on the demonic? Late in the evening, when the light disappears and the darkness envelops your prone form, has the thought of wicked wisps whirling about you never prevailed? Surely in a rash of nervousness, you have ushered such thoughts away from your waking mind, lest your imagination terrorize you and steal your rest? If this fright is a common feeling, why then would we bother raising the subject? Why would we gaze at the Scriptures concerning such fearsome matters? John Calvin offers us solace by denoting the profits of our journey:

> The tendency of all that Scripture teaches concerning devils [demons] is to put us on our guard against their wiles and machinations, that we may provide ourselves with weapons strong enough to drive out the most formidable foes. For when Satan is called the god and ruler of this world, the strong man armed, the prince of the power of the air, the roaring lion, the object of all these descriptions is to make us more cautious and vigilant, and more prepared for the contest. . . . Being forewarned of the constant presence of an enemy . . . let us not allow ourselves to be overtaken by sloth or cowardice, but, on the contrary, with minds aroused and ever on the alert, let us stand ready to resist; and, knowing that this warfare is terminated only by death, let us study to persevere. Above all, fully conscious of our weakness and want of skill, let us invoke the help of God, and attempt nothing without trusting in him, since it is his alone to supply counsel, and strength, and courage, and arms.[1]

---

1. John Calvin, *Institutes of the Christian Religion* (Grand Rapids: Eerdmans, 1970), Book 1, XIV, Section 13, 150–51.

So then, let us ask questions with force and purpose! What is the demonic? How should we speak about demons? What impact do they have in the world? These questions occur naturally within the hearts of many, including Christians. But these questions are not mere thoughts of idle curiosity. These chapters delving into the content of demonology are not unimportant explorations. For the Christian church on this groaning globe, we are bound by necessity and implored to bravery . . . "let us study to persevere."

Contrary to the tradition of many demonologies, we will begin by analyzing the behavior of demonic beings. While many writings prioritize the origin and nature of demonic beings, Holy Scripture does not share that priority. In fact, the biblical authors do not concern themselves with an ontological study of demonic beings nor with precise definitions of their abilities and attributes. Demonic beings are introduced by their behavior, especially in their relationship to God's plan of human redemption and the experiences of God's elect. They are actors in supporting roles who are not afforded a wealth of scripted character development. Recall the contributions of the accuser in Job 1:6–12:

> Now there was a day when the sons of God came to present themselves before the LORD, and Satan also came among them. The LORD said to Satan, "From where do you come?" Satan answered the LORD and said, "From roaming about on the earth and walking around on it." The LORD said to Satan, "Have you considered My servant Job? For there is no one like him on the earth, a blameless and upright man, fearing God and turning away from evil." Then Satan answered the LORD, "Does Job fear God for nothing? Have You not made a fence about him and his house and all that he has, on every side? You have blessed the work of his hands, and his possessions have increased in the land. But reach out with Your hand now and touch all that he has; he will certainly curse You to Your face." Then the LORD said to Satan, "Behold, all that he has is in your power; only do not reach out and put your hand on him." So Satan departed from the presence of the LORD.[2]

The scene is indicative of the role of the demonic in general and of Satan in particular. The emphasis is not Satan or his character. Rather the Lord orchestrates, Satan acts, and Job suffers.

---

2. Satan's activity, accusing, is on full display, and this activity is what defines his character. "The Satan (or the Accuser) represented those who opposed God and his good people. In Job the Satan assumed his classical pose of charging a good man with evil (Rev 12:10)." Alden, *Job*, 54.

Shall we then skip a discussion of the nature of the demonic? Absolutely not. But with the text's preoccupation with the activity of demons and Satan, we instead will assess the biblical depiction of ten of their behaviors, letting that information instruct our perspective of demonic origins and identity. If we reverse the order, we are more susceptible to imposing our presuppositions upon the nature of the demonic. From this erroneous vantage point, we would then filter all accounts of demonic behavior through a faulty interpretive lens.

Deception

Having summarized how we will organize the biblical material concerning the demonic, we will now discuss the first of ten behaviors of demons. The actions of Satan and his fallen comrades appear at the beginning of human existence. Imagine that as we stride through Eden, we can hear a disturbance. Armed with lies, the serpent's entrance shatters the idyllic paradise.

> Now the serpent was more cunning than any animal of the field which the LORD God had made. And he said to the woman, "Has God really said, 'You shall not eat from any tree of the garden'?" The woman said to the serpent, "From the fruit of the trees of the garden we may eat; but from the fruit of the tree which is in the middle of the garden, God has said, 'You shall not eat from it or touch it, or you will die.'" The serpent said to the woman, "You certainly will not die! For God knows that on the day you eat from it your eyes will be opened, and you will become like God, knowing good and evil." (Gen 3:1–5)[3]

No demonic origins are evident, and the explanation of this visitation is minimal. Apart from the full counsel of Scripture, a casual reader could conclude that the serpent mentioned in this Genesis narrative was little more

---

3. Kenneth Mathews states,
> Although the origin of the snake is attributed to God, there is no attempt here to explain the origins of evil. The narrative explains only the origin of human sin and guilt. There is no explanation for the serpent's capacity to talk other than possibly that it was "crafty." It is assumed that the animal has this ability, and the fact that the woman did not find this alarming only heightens the suspicion that the serpent is representative of something or someone sinisterly powerful. In any case the substance of what the serpent says is more important than who or what the serpent is.

Kenneth A. Mathews, *Genesis 1–11:26*, New American Commentary (Nashville: B & H, 1996), 232.

than a stray beast that wandered into the garden. But as Kenneth Mathews says, one's suspicion of "something or someone sinisterly powerful" is aroused by the actions of this talking snake.[4] Jesus's statement about Satan in the Gospel of John rings true. As Jesus responds to those who rejected him, he concludes, "You are of your father the devil, and you want to do the desires of your father. He was a murderer from the beginning, and does not stand in the truth because there is no truth in him. Whenever he speaks a lie, he speaks from his own nature, for he is a liar and the father of lies" (John 8:44).[5] Jesus authoritatively references the initial and ongoing "ministry" of the devil, which the opponents of Jesus emulate. As George Beasley-Murray notes, "They carry out what [the devil] wants, and that above all is to kill, for (*a*) he was a murderer from the beginning, (*b*) he is a liar, and (*c*) he is the father of lying. The saying reflects the narrative of the fall in Gen 3."[6] The interpretation is straightforward: Jesus

---

4. Mathews, *Genesis 1–11:26*, 232. While we cannot know for certain if Satan used an animal in this text, examples of supernatural and animal interactions are present in the Bible but irregular. One famous case involves the corrupt prophet Balaam and the angel of the Lord in Num 22:22–35. Cole comments,

> Upon each of three occasions the donkey evidences clear perception of the appearance of the messenger from the Lord, and she turns aside presumably in fear of [her] life.... God's intervention takes on extraordinary proportions through the opening of the heretofore unintelligible mouth of a lowly female donkey who is enabled to communicate with a human, and through the unveiling of the eyes of an incognizant prophet whose training and expertise in the ways of deity had not equipped him to see the divine representative standing directly in front of him.

R. Dennis Cole, *Numbers*, New American Commentary (Nashville: B & H, 2000), 390–91. Yet when we are searching for overt cases of demonic relationships with the animal kingdom, we are drawn to Mark's account of the Gerasene demoniac, wherein the demonic legion requests a transfer into a nearby herd of swine. Geulich writes,

> Like the description of the unmanageable man in [Mark] 5:3–4, whose behavior "Legion" helps explain, 2000 uncontrollable swine demonstrate the immense power of the forces that had taken control of their victim. Furthermore, the death of the swine vividly depicts the destructive nature of these evil forces. From the beginning, however, these unclean spirits had recognized and submitted themselves to Jesus' authority.

Guelich, *Mark 1–8:26*, 282. However, no biblical instance seems to neatly mirror the events of Genesis 3.

5. Lenski states, "The devil's children always actually will and go on willing ... to do or to carry into action ... these lusts. The evil desire kindled in the heart gives birth to the corresponding deed. No evil deed is without this evil root. Thus the deed is prima facie proof first of the lusts, secondly of the inward connection with the devil." Lenski, *Interpretation of St. John's Gospel*, 649.

6. George R. Beasley-Murray, *John* (Waco, TX: Word, 1987), 135. While it could be argued that Satan's violent fatherhood is first seen in Cain's murder of Abel, death itself is inaugurated due to Satan's garden deception. In that sense, Satan was a murderer prior to Cain, for all human death sprung from his lie.

understood that the original deception had its origin in the devil, and the serpent was an instrument of that deception.

The Genesis 3 text alone unveils the patterns of demonic behavior. First, Satan appears. While the possibility exists that he inhabited a snake (Gen 2:19; 3:1; "animal of the field"), another option is that one of Satan's forms is a snake-like dragon. Depictions of heavenly beings with animal-like features occur throughout Scripture, and ancient cultures also attest to similar angelic beings.[7] Second, the antagonist corrupted and bent God's "very good" creation (1:31) to wicked ends. Third, Satan lied when he claimed that Eve would not die (3:4). Fourth, he deceived her by misrepresenting the consequences of disobeying God (3:5). The eyes of Adam and Eve would be opened, but the knowledge gained would not be beneficial to them. Fifth, the devil introduced skepticism regarding the intentions of God and his divine commands. Satan stimulated doubt. As Mathew says, "The tactic used by the serpent was to cause doubt in the mind of the woman through interrogation and misrepresentation."[8] Sixth, the sum of all of Satan's efforts was a full-fledged rebellion against the Creator. Humanity, created in the image of God, was deceived.

Deception is the foremost evil of the demonic upon which are founded all its other works. Satanic power and falsehood mislead, obscuring the truth. Under the dominion of the devil, "the deceiver of the whole world" (Rev 12:9), humanity is blinded. Paul states, "And even if our gospel is veiled, it is veiled to those who are perishing, in whose case the god of this world has blinded the minds of the unbelieving so that they might not see the light of the gospel of the glory of Christ, who is the image of God" (2 Cor 4:3–4).[9] Truth is the ultimate foe of Satan and his host, and therefore, these dishonest ones oppose, obscure and drown it out.

---

7. Heiser, *Demons*, 66.
8. Mathews, *Genesis 1–11:26*, 234.
9. David Garland states,
> Paul blames another influence for the failure to believe: The god of this age has blinded the minds of unbelievers. The phrase "god of this age" occurs only here in the New Testament, and most understand it as a reference to Satan. . . . If Paul were actually referring to God here, it is strange that he does not characterize him as the God of all ages rather than simply the God of this age. Paul must be referring to Satan as the god of this age. He classifies Satan as a "god" because he has a dominion, however limited by the one true God, and has subjects whom Paul labels "unbelievers." Paul portrays the archenemy Satan as blinding unbelievers' minds.

David E. Garland, *2 Corinthians*, New American Commentary (Nashville: B & H, 1999), 211.

Like Eve's doctrinal recitation in the garden, a stampede of satanic lies and deceptions trample over the truth. But not all demonic deception is stark. First Timothy 4:1–2 warns us about the subtle work of false teaching, "But the Spirit explicitly says that in later times some will fall away from the faith, paying attention to deceitful spirits and doctrines of demons, by means of the hypocrisy of liars seared in their own conscience as with a branding iron."[10] Kato comments on this text, "The evil spirits have a set of false teachings that they spread. Such false teachings are even spread by some Bible teachers."[11] Paul warns that the enemy has an interest in undermining the corporate body of believers through false teachers who promote false doctrines. What some might mistake as mere religious division was actually demonic according to Paul. Paul "also saw behind the activity of his opponents in Corinth the work of Satan."[12] With a similar call for discernment pertaining to spiritual instruction, John implores us to "test the spirits," lest we too become an instrument of demonic dogma (1 John 4:1). "His warning is clear: behind every statement is a spirit . . . but not every spirit is the Spirit of God."[13] In this way, we, churches and individuals, are in conflict with demonic powers for the preservation and propagation of the truth.

With all this deception, whom are we to trust? In a world deceived by the beguiling tricks of the demonic, only divine revelation can offer us certainty.

Corruption

The activity of the demons – unclean spirits – did not end in the garden. In Genesis 6, a mysterious reference to the "sons of God" appears. Wickedness was rife throughout humanity at that time. Genesis testifies "that every intent of the thoughts of their hearts was only evil continually" (Gen 6:5). But was the demonic involved in this moral decline? Mathews surveys the various positions concerning the sons of God and their role.

---

10. Lenski asserts, "This is a genitive of source: doctrines that emanate from demons, and not the objective genitive: doctrines about demons, the latter the Scriptures themselves contain . . . . We need not puzzle our minds about the occult activity of demons; the antichristian doctrines betray their origin all too plainly." R. C. H. Lenski, *The Interpretation of St. Paul's Epistles to the Colossians, to the Thessalonians, to Timothy, to Titus and to Philemon* (Minneapolis: Augsburg, 1961), 619.

11. Byang Kato, *What the Bible Teaches: The Spirits* (Achimota, Ghana: Africa Christian, 1975), 19.

12. Martin Dibelius and Hans Conzelmann, *The Pastoral Epistles: A Commentary on the Pastoral Epistles*, Hermeneia (Philadelphia: Fortress, 1972), 64.

13. Daniel L. Akin, *1, 2, 3 John*, New American Commentary (Nashville: B & H, 2001), 170.

Historically, three opinions have won a significant following for identifying the "sons of God": (1) angels, (2) human judges or rulers, and (3) the descendants of Seth. More recently some have suggested that this baffling epithet refers to royal despots, similar to the second view. Others have taken a combination of the angel and human views in which the human despots are demoniacs possessed by fallen angels.[14]

Dickason's opinion on the matter is well put, as he simplifies the interpretations to two, humans or angels. "Either view has its problems, and good men are divided on the question."[15]

Let us therefore speak lightly, not presuming to settle the dispute with a few paragraphs. But the weight of canonical evidence pushes us away from a purely humanistic interpretation. In a brief, nonspeculative manner, here are some reasons why we should advocate for the positions of demonized rulers or actualized demonic powers.[16] First, the phrase "sons of God" is telling. "It is true that outside of Genesis 6 the exact term 'the sons of God' (*bene elohim*) is used only of angels (Job 1:6; 2:1; 38:7)."[17]

Second, in Matthew 22:30, Jesus does not specifically state that fallen, earth-dwelling angels cannot marry or engage in a sexual relationship. He says, "For in the resurrection they neither marry nor are given in marriage, but are like angels in heaven." Because of the locative phrase "in heaven," sexual deviancy is a possibility for impure angels who have left their proper place. Instead angelic beings in human form, as in case of the angels who visited Lot (Genesis 19:1–11), or demonized humans would be capable of sexual behavior since they can participate in the physical realm.[18]

Third, the testimonies of 2 Peter 2:4–6 and Jude 6–7 guide us toward the historical reality of licentious transgressions – sexual sins – by celestial powers.

> For if God did not spare angels when they sinned, but cast them into hell and committed them to pits of darkness, held for judgment; and did not spare the ancient world, but protected Noah, a preacher of righteousness, with seven others, when He brought a flood upon the world of the ungodly; and if He

---

14. Mathews, *Genesis 1–11:26*, 325.
15. Dickason, *Angels*, 222.
16. The term "actualized" refers to a spiritual being appearing and interacting in the physical realm. Actualized is also distinct from "incarnated," since demons are not human.
17. Dickason, 223.
18. For example, angels ate with Abram (Gen 18).

> condemned the cities of Sodom and Gomorrah to destruction by reducing them to ashes, having made them an example of what is coming for the ungodly. (2 Pet 2:4–6)[19]
>
> And angels who did not keep their own domain, but abandoned their proper dwelling, these He has kept in eternal restraints under darkness for the judgment of the great day, just as Sodom and Gomorrah and the cities around them, since they in the same way as these angels indulged in sexual perversion and went after strange flesh, are exhibited as an example in undergoing the punishment of eternal fire. (Jude 6–7)

Peter and Jude affirm that Genesis 6 depicts the sexual sin of fallen angels. Jude links the promiscuity of Sodom and Gomorrah to the behavior of these demons, and God exhibited stringent justice to these parties to provide a warning of judgment to us today.

Does the testimony of Peter and Jude validate the entirety of 1 Enoch and Jewish tradition? Schreiner asserts the following:

> The second example of judgment involves the angels who sinned. We have already noted that Jewish tradition linked together the sin of angels in Gen 6:1–4, the judgment of Sodom and Gomorrah, and the punishment of the wilderness generation. We can be almost certain that Jude referred here to the sin of the angels in Gen 6:1–4. The sin the angels committed, according to the Jewish tradition, was sexual intercourse with the daughters of men. Apparently Jude also understood Gen 6:1–4 in the same way. Three reasons support such a conclusion. First, Jewish tradition consistently understood Gen 6:1–4 in this way. . . . Second, we know from vv. 14–15 that Jude was influenced by 1 Enoch, and 1 Enoch goes into great detail about the sin and punishment of these angels. Jude almost certainly would need to explain that he departed from the customary

---

19. Schreiner states,

> The first judgment relates to the angels whom God did not spare when they sinned. Peter differed from Jude in that he emphasized the judgment without giving specifics of the angels' sin. Some scholars in the history of interpretation have identified this as the prehistoric fall of angels. It is doubtful, however, that Peter referred to this event in this particular text, even if it is a legitimate deduction theologically. Instead, we can be almost certain that Peter followed Jewish tradition at this point and referred to the sin angels committed with women in Gen 6:1–4.

Schreiner, *1, 2 Peter, Jude*, 334.

Jewish view of Gen 6:1–4 if he disagreed with Jewish tradition. The brevity of the verse supports the idea that he concurred with Jewish tradition. Third, the text forges a parallel between the sin of Sodom and Gomorrah and the angels.... The implication is that sexual sin was prominent in both instances.[20]

It seems beyond debate that "The author of the Epistle of Jude has an especially close relationship to Enochic and other noncanonical traditions."[21] But concerning Jude's relationship to 1 Enoch, the supposition that Jude was treating 1 Enoch as canon is without basis. While the later citation of 1 Enoch is intriguing, Jude does not affirm the entire contents of 1 Enoch, and he cites only the most canonically consistent portions of 1 Enoch. In sum, Jude 5–7 likely accepts the historic, Jewish understanding of Genesis 6:1–4 instead of providing a comprehensive approval of 1 Enoch's speculative and elaborative contents. "We must be careful, however, to avoid saying that Jude necessarily agreed with everything found in *1 Enoch* or Jewish tradition in general. His own reference to the tradition is terse and avoids the kind of speculation we find in *1 Enoch* 6–8."[22]

The demonic activity in the period before the flood accelerated humanity's complete corruption. Of course, God proved himself faithful through Noah and the single family of righteousness, but Erwin Lutzer's description of the ancient time is fitting. He prefers to presume that the demons inhabited people to accomplish their aims.

> These evil angels left their abode and inhabited bodies of human warriors, the mighty ones of the earth. These mighty rulers were not divine, nor were they the offspring of the gods (as often believed in pagan religions.) Instead, these ... were ordinary human beings given superhuman strength because they were demonically controlled. They lived lives of rampant sexuality and violence. They married as many women as they wished and engaged in all manner of sexual perversion. The children of these marriages were not god-kings, but men of flesh and blood who eventually died in the flood.[23]

---

20. Schreiner, 447.
21. George W. E. Nickelsburg and Klaus Baltzer, *1 Enoch: A Commentary on the Book of 1 Enoch*, Hermeneia (Minneapolis: Fortress, 2001), 86.
22. Schreiner, *1, 2 Peter, Jude*, 450.
23. Erwin W. Lutzer, *God's Devil* (Chicago: Moody, 1996), 92.

Surely such a scene of corruption, whether demons inhabited people or physically manifested to enable human interaction, would require a dramatic intervention of divine wrath.

Dominion

After God's dramatic reordering of the earth by the flood, Noah and his offspring repopulated a refreshed creation with new boundaries. They were required by God to fill the earth (Gen 9:1), but widespread rebellion stirred yet again at the tower of Babel. God intervened and so birthed the table of nations in Genesis 10. God's judgment forged diversity, "setting the table" for his long-term salvation purposes.

But what does all of this have to do with the demonic? The division and establishment of the nations appears in the song of Moses. It says:

> When the Most High gave the nations their inheritance,
> When He separated the sons of mankind,
> He set the boundaries of the peoples
> According to the number of the sons of Israel.
> For the LORD's portion is His people;
> Jacob is the allotment of His inheritance. (Deut 32:8–9)[24]

The phrase "according to the number of the sons of Israel" (32:8) does not seem to fit logically. How did God set up nations in accordance with a people group that did not exist at that time? A textual issue is apparent, since other translations say "sons of God" (ESV) or "heavenly court" (NLT). The correct reading is "sons of God," as the Septuagint (LXX) and Qumran manuscripts show.[25] Heiser comments, "Although some may fear that to adopt the reading of the LXX amounts to embracing the notion that Yahweh is the author of polytheism, nothing could be further from the truth. In fact, a proper understanding of the concept of the divine council in the Old Testament provides a decisive argument in favor of the LXX / Qumran reading."[26] In other words, God instituted an angelic host to oversee the affairs of the nations

---

24. Eugene Merrill states, "The point of departure was when the Most High ... divided humankind into nations and assigned to them their geographical and historical allotments (v. 8a). This act of universal sovereignty supplies clear evidence of the Lord's concern for the whole world, his special selection of Israel notwithstanding." Eugene H. Merrill, *Deuteronomy*, New American Commentary (Nashville: B & H, 1994), 413. Unfortunately, Merrill does not interact with the textual debate and instead comments in line with the Hebrew Masoretic text reading.

25. Michael S. Heiser, "Deuteronomy 32:8 and the Sons of God," *The Divine Council*.

26. Heiser, "Deuteronomy 32:8 and the Sons of God," 8.

by shaping their cultures, religions, and politics. The sons of God received dominion over their respective realms while the Lord specifically called Israel to be his own people. The division of humanity in Genesis 10 also determined the distribution of spiritual beings and their national assignments. Newsom helpfully summarizes, "According to Deut 32:8 (LXX and 4QDeut), when God organized the political structure of the world, each of the nations was assigned to one of the angels/minor deities, with Israel reserved for Yahweh's own possession."[27]

We have affirmed that supernatural powers have dominion over the various nations of the earth. But are these unseen rulers actually demons? Yes. The rest of Scripture supports that demons continue to serve as ruling powers in the created realm. First, the testimony of Daniel is critical. After a terrifying vision, Daniel receives comfort, and in a narrative dialogue, an angel states the following:

> Do not be afraid, Daniel, for from the first day that you set your heart on understanding this and on humbling yourself before your God, your words were heard, and I have come in response to your words. But the prince of the kingdom of Persia was standing in my way for twenty-one days; then behold, Michael, one of the chief princes, came to help me, for I had been left there with the kings of Persia. Now I have come to explain to you of what will happen to your people in the latter days, for the vision pertains to the days still future. . . .
>
> Do you understand why I came to you? But I shall now return to fight against the prince of Persia; so I am leaving, and behold, the prince of Greece is about to come. (Dan 10:12–14, 20)

While we cannot entertain the many questions which arise from this text, we must ask, who are these princes? They are the spiritual rulers over the various nations, and they are in conflict with one another. One commentary plainly states, "The prince of the kingdom of Persia: This indicated the patron angel of Persia."[28] Unbeknownst to Daniel, unseen forces were battling as he prayed, and these angels, except for Michael and Gabriel, do not appear to be holy angels who minister to God's people. Rather, they are corrupt powers placed over the nations.

---

27. Newsom, "Angels," 249.

28. John Joseph Collins, Frank Moore Cross, and Adela Yarbro Collins, *Daniel: A Commentary on the Book of Daniel*, Hermeneia (Minneapolis: Fortress, 1993), 374.

Second, the Scriptures also depict the divine council, wherein the sons of God – good and evil spirits – convene in the heavenly presence of God. These powers can even enter the human realm. Observe these scenes from Job and 1 Kings:

> Now there was a day when the sons of God came to present themselves before the LORD, and Satan also came among them. . . .
> Again, there was a day when the sons of God came to present themselves before the LORD, and Satan also came among them to present himself before the LORD. (Job 1:6; 2:1)[29]

> Micaiah said, "Therefore, hear the word of the LORD. I saw the LORD sitting on His throne, and all the angels of heaven standing by Him on His right and on His left. The LORD said, 'Who will entice Ahab to go up and fall at Ramoth-gilead?' And one spirit said this while another said that. Then a spirit came forward and stood before the LORD, and said, 'I will entice him.' The LORD said to him, 'How?' And he said, 'I will go out and be a deceiving spirit in the mouths of all his prophets.' Then He said, 'You shall entice him, and you will also prevail. Go and do so.'" (1 Kgs 22:19–22)[30]

While many are familiar with the story of Job, the prophetic utterance of Micaiah is less familiar yet more detailed. Apparently, the spirits, both the wicked and the virtuous, gather before God. God's sovereign purposes for them are varied, but they can enact testing, as in the case of Job, and judgment, as in the case of Ahab. By extension, we should not be surprised that God would delegate these fallen powers to rule nations, though they still operate as servants in God's monotheistic universe. Lest someone accuse this perspective of being a form of polytheism, Ferdinando's assertion is correct: "Yahweh's council is simply a forum in which he conveys orders and executes judgement, not a council of gods."[31]

---

29. According to Alden, "The 'sons of God' are both plural and inferior to God. . . . Apparently God has a council or cabinet . . . Not every one of them is good because 1 Kings 22:20–23 speaks of a 'spirit' willing to be a 'lying spirit in the mouths of all [Ahab's] prophets.' The Satan was among them or perhaps even their leader." Alden, *Job*, 53.

30. Paul House states, "As in earlier difficult passages in the former prophets (e.g. 1 Sam 16:13–14; 2 Sam 24:1–17) this text focuses on God's sovereignty. Nothing escapes the Lord's notice, and no one operates outside of the Lord's jurisdiction." Paul R. House, *1, 2 Kings*, New American Commentary (Nashville: B & H, 1995), 237.

31. Ferdinando, *Triumph of Christ in African Perspective*, 143.

This pair of passages also serves to clarify the demonic quality of the fallen sons of God. If anyone argues that an ontological distinction exists between the sons of God and the evil spirits (demons), the combination of Job 1 and 1 Kings 22 dispels that notion. The assembly is "all the angels of heaven," synonymous with "the sons of God." This council consists of spiritual beings created by God. In 1 Kings 22, one of the members of the host called a "spirit" acts in the manner of a demon by spreading deceit on earth. And Satan, surely one of the fallen members of the council, inhabits Judas just as a New Testament demon does (John 13:27). Therefore, by behavior, it is unwise to insist that the sons of God and the demonic host are two separate groups. Such an argument does not naturally arise from Scripture. Rather, the sons of God who exert dominion over the nations are demons.

Third, the New Testament also employs heavenly and authoritarian terminology concerning evil spiritual powers. Ephesians 6:11–12 articulates this heavenly hierarchy:

> Put on the full armor of God, so that you will be able to stand firm against the schemes of the devil. For our struggle is not against flesh and blood, but against the rulers, against the powers, against the world forces of this darkness, against the spiritual forces of wickedness in the heavenly places.[32]

Jesus Christ won salvation at the cross, yet the struggle against demonic forces is ongoing. In the process of living wisely in Christ's service, we resist these powers who oversee the nations.

The dominion of the demonic continues today. The pivotal work of Christ has "'put aside' the old order of the rulers and authorities; he 'stripped' them of their authority."[33] The Lord of the invisible realm has rendered the gods illegitimate, yet the demonic powers of the nations still await judgment. In ages past, God claimed one nation while consigning the rest of the nations to their

---

32. Andrew Lincoln states,
> Here "the devil" is singled out as the primary enemy, the chief of the opposing army, so that the forces of evil which lie behind human activity are seen as having a personal center. . . . The term . . . "world rulers" originated in astrological discussion where it referred to the planets and their determination of human fate and world affairs. . . . Also in the magical papyri, gods such as Sarapis and Hermes are called world rulers, and the use of this term for evil spirit powers here may indicate that the writer shares the view of Paul in 1 Corinthians 10:20 that pagan gods are closely linked with demonic forces.

Andrew T. Lincoln, *Ephesians* (Dallas: Word, 1990), 443–44.

33. Heiser, *Demons*, 229.

demonic overlords. Currently, we live in an epoch in which the rule of Christ is expanding among the nations, unveiling the weakness of the spiritual rulers.

False Worship and Occultism

After the dispersion of humanity from the tower of Babel, the activity of demons not only extended over the nations but also over the false worship which permeated human culture. People from every territory worshipped various gods, represented by idols which were the product of human craftmanship. Yet the one true God had the Israelites, and their invisible God was a stark contrast to the idols of the nations.[34] The Ten Commandments strictly forbids the worship of false gods and the creation of idols. The Lord says, "You shall have no other gods before Me. You shall not make for yourself an idol, or any likeness of what is in heaven above or on the earth beneath, or in the water under the earth. You shall not worship them or serve them" (Exod 20:3–5a).[35] But what do idolatry and false gods have to do with demons?

Before we answer that question, let us take a moment to review a small portion of the cultural context that Douglas Stuart describes in his commentary on Exodus.

> Ancients assumed that the presence of a god or goddess was guaranteed by the presence of an idol since the idol "partook" of the very essence of the divinity it was designed to represent. When, for example, a statue of a given god was carved and certain ritual incantations spoken over that statue to cause the essence of the god to enter it, the statue was then understood to become a functioning conduit for anything done in its presence from the worshiper to that god.[36]

---

34. See Ps 115 for one biblical example of the distinction between God and idols.
35. Douglas Stuart says,
    Why, then, did God not just say, "I am the only God. Don't believe in any others"? The answer is, as previously noted, to be found in the range of meaning of the term [gods]. The word . . . carries the connotation of "supernatural beings," including angels. Accordingly, this first word/commandment implicitly acknowledges that there are many "gods" (nonhuman, nonearthly beings) in the same sense that Ps 82 does (or that Jesus does in John 10:34–36) but at the same time demands that only Yahweh be worshiped as the sole divinity, or God. All other "gods" (supernatural beings such as angels) are to be understood and appreciated for their roles in the universe, but only Yahweh is divine.
    Douglas K. Stuart, *Exodus*, New American Commentary (Nashville: B & H, 2006), 449.
36. Stuart, *Exodus*, 450.

Stuart introduces us to the concept of idols as conduits, and that understanding is helpful as we consider the role that demons play in idolatry.

As strange as it seems to those who embrace the idea that all faiths are equally valid, the Scriptures portray false gods and idols as demonic. First, when discussing eating meat sacrificed to idols, Paul explains demonic involvement.

> What do I mean then? That a thing sacrificed to idols is anything, or that an idol is anything? No, but I say that the things which the Gentiles sacrifice, they sacrifice to demons and not to God; and I do not want you to become sharers in demons. You cannot drink the cup of the Lord and the cup of demons; you cannot partake of the table of the Lord and the table of demons. (1 Cor 10:19–21)[37]

The actual idols are nothing, meaningless, and empty. They are simply material objects. Yet something stands behind these idols; the idols are a conduit to the evil supernatural beings who reside among us and assemble in the heavens.

Second, Paul's declaration reflects the song of Moses in Deuteronomy 32 and the testimony of Psalm 106.[38] Continuing our previous discussion of Deuteronomy 32, we move onward from verse eight to verse seventeen. In reference to the religious rebellion of Israel, the passage reads, "They sacrificed to demons, who were not God, to gods whom they have not known, new gods who came lately, whom your fathers did not know" (Deut 32:17).[39] When the Israelites abandoned the worship of the Lord and selfishly pursued the gods of the Gentiles (i.e. the sons of God of 32:8), they were offering sacrifices to demonic powers.[40]

---

37. Conzelmann states, "The presupposition of vv 19–20 is the same as of 8:5: behind the gods there lurk demons. Paul bases this view on Deut 32:17. This makes his demand clear. Sacrifices would make the demons into gods, powers, and bring the participants into bondage to them." Hans Conzelmann, *1 Corinthians: A Commentary on the First Epistle to the Corinthians*, Hermeneia (Philadelphia: Fortress, 1975), 173.

38. Ps 106:37 says, "They even sacrificed their sons and their daughters to the demons." Ps 96:5 is a similar but debated reference. "For all the gods of the peoples are idols, but the LORD made the heavens." The Septuagint renders "idols" as "demons," since the essence of the Hebrew word "denotes weak/insufficient/worthless things." Marvin E. Tate, *Psalms 51-100* (Nashville: Thomas Nelson, 2003), 510.

39. Ferdinando advocates that this text (along with Ps 106:37) is one of the few Old Testament cases which references demons with "any certainty." Ferdinando, *Triumph of Christ*, 151.

40. While experiences are not a primary guide, we will include one case from the research of John Nevius. Rev J. Innocent, who served with a Methodist mission in China, sent a letter to Nevius on 1 February 1881. Here is the account he shared,

Third, Paul's epistle to the Galatians also discusses the subject of supernatural powers. In chapter 4, he writes concerning the state of the Galatians' bondage before they came to Christ:

> So we too, when we were children, were held in bondage under the elementary principles of the world. . . . However at that time, when you did not know God, you were slaves to those which by nature are not gods. But now that you have come to know God, or rather to be known by God, how is it that you turn back again to the weak and worthless elementary principles, to which you want to be enslaved all over again? (Gal 4:3, 8–9)[41]

Human beings, apart from the knowledge of God through Christ, are "held in bondage under the elementary principles of the world" (Gal 4:3). Clinton Arnold identifies these "elementary principles" as "evil demonic powers of the same category as the hostile 'principalities and powers.'"[42] Therefore in Galatians, Paul describes the demonic slavery of the Galatian believers' former religious order. The false gods of the nations, "those which by nature are not gods" (Gal 4:8), imposed this system. Paul's concern is obvious. Surely having experienced the adoption of God as his children, these believers would not reclaim the oppression of their former overlords! Following the example of Jesus in Matthew 4:9–10, Christians then and now must reject the worship of Satan and all other false gods.

> In the village Yang-kialo, there is a family named Yang, in which a woman was grievously tormented by evil spirits, and had been for fifteen years. She frequently appeared on the streets declaring to the people that the teachings of the Christian religion came from heaven; and that men ought to believe and reverence this religion. She was asked: "Has not the Mi-mi religion (a local sect) power to cast you out?" She replied: "The Mi-mi kiao is a religion of demons; how could it cast me out? I am also a demon (mokwei)."

Nevius, *Demon Possession*, 19.

41. Arnold states,

> In Gal. 4:8, Paul compares the *stoicheia* with beings that the pagans regard as gods. In denying that these beings are gods, Paul is not denying that they have a real existence, only their claim to be gods. Paul expressed a similar idea to the Corinthians when he noted that there are many entities "called gods" . . . to whom sacrifices are made (1 Cor. 8:5) whom he subsequently identifies as evil demons (1 Cor. 10:19–20).

Clinton Arnold, "Returning to the Domain of the Powers: *Stoicheia* as Evil Spirits in Galatians 4:3, 9," *Novum Testamentum* 38, no. 1 (1996): 60.

42. Arnold, "Returning to the Domain," 63.

How does this discussion about false religion, the gods of the nations, and the demonic relate to occultism? Let us begin by defining occultism. The *Evangelical Dictionary of Theology* says:

> Those phenomena collectively known as "the occult" may be said to have the following distinct characteristics: (1) the disclosure and communication of information unavailable to humans through normal means (beyond the five senses); (2) the placing of persons in contact with supernatural powers, paranormal energies, or demonic forces; (3) the acquisition and mastery of power in order to manipulate or influence other people into certain actions.[43]

A complete survey of the innumerable occult practices is not possible in this work, but we can comment on the interrelationship between occultism and the demonic.

Occultism is an extension of false religion because it represents a rebellious rejection of God's provision and looks elsewhere for supernatural power and knowledge. All false worship is occultism, and all occultism is in some sense false religion, except that occultism tends to be more personal and less institutional. Of course, this statement does not deny the varieties or distinctions between them! But when we sort through the claims of false religions and occult practices, the same "benefits" and features permeate both to varying degrees.

Do the Scriptures portray occultism as demonic? While the Bible soundly condemns occultism of every kind, it only briefly describes beings in the demonic realm as the animating forces behind it. Remembering our previous identification of the demonic with the gods of the nations, there are a few texts for us to consider. First, in the showdown between the God of Israel and the gods of Egypt, dueling works are on display in Exodus 7. When Moses and Aaron performed one supernatural act, such as a staff transforming into a snake or water turning into blood, the Egyptian magicians replicated it (Exod 7:10–11, 20–22). While it is possible that these magicians were charlatans performing illusions,[44] the scene links the occult practices of the magicians to

---

43. R. M. Enroth, "The Occult," in *Evangelical Dictionary of Theology*, ed. Walter A. Elwell (Grand Rapids: Baker Book House, 1984), 787.

44. Stuart asserts that the magicians employed trickery instead of "any supernatural means." Stuart, *Exodus*, 194. However, the transformed staff presents a difficulty for that hypothesis.

the false gods of Egypt. (The story of Simon the magician in Acts 8 is similar.[45]) Since we affirm that false religion is empowered by demons, Exodus 7 should at least implicate the deception of magic as demonic.

Second, look at the reasons for the fall of the northern kingdom of Israel in 2 Kings.

> And they abandoned all the commandments of the LORD their God and made for themselves cast metal images: two calves. And they made an Asherah, and worshiped all the heavenly lights, and served Baal. Then they made their sons and their daughters pass through the fire, and they practiced divination and interpreting omens, and gave themselves over to do evil in the sight of the LORD, provoking Him. (2 Kgs 17:16–17)[46]

No debate exists about the wickedness of Israel at that time! But as we ponder the relationship between occultism and the demonic, the author of 2 Kings provides evidence of the link. In this analysis of Israel's sins, the worship of false gods, including human sacrifice, partners with "divination and interpreting omens." Since the worship of such gods is demonic, occult practices and demons are certainly overlapped or at least somewhat associated in this text.

Third, the most decisive link between occultism and demonic activity is in Acts 16. The apostle Paul confronts a demonized slave girl who possessed supernatural powers of foretelling the future.

> It happened that as we were going to the place of prayer, a slave woman who had a spirit of divination met us, who was bringing great profit to her masters by fortune-telling. She followed Paul and us and cried out repeatedly saying, "These men are bond-servants of the Most High God, who are proclaiming to you the way of salvation." Now she continued doing this for many days.

---

45. According to Lenski, "This Simon belonged to a class of charlatans that were rather common at this period, who practiced occult arts in order to impress the people and to gain a following. Much was plain sorcery which was at times combined with a shrewd use of natural laws that were otherwise unknown." R. C. H. Lenski, *The Interpretation of the Acts of the Apostles* (Minneapolis: Augsburg, 1961), 318–19.

46. House states,

> The writer's frustration is evident as the summary continues. Israel has imitated the worst tradition of their fathers and "rejected his decrees and the covenant" (v. 15). They practiced worship rites connected with pagan deities. More specifically, they bowed down before Baal and the Canaanite astral gods. Some of them offered human sacrifices. In short, "They followed worthless idols and themselves became worthless."

House, *1, 2, Kings*, 341.

> But Paul was greatly annoyed, and he turned and said to the spirit, "I command you in the name of Jesus Christ to come out of her!" And it came out at that very moment. (Acts 16:16–18)

In this narrative, we perceive the underlying connections between occultism, false religion, and demonic powers. The apostle Paul treats this fortune-telling girl like any other demoniac by performing an exorcism in keeping with the model of Christ. Yet as John Polhill states, the term for the spirit she has, a python spirit, ties into the pagan religion of that region. He says,

> On one of the occasions when the four missionaries were going outside the city to the place of prayer, they were encountered by a slave girl who had a spirit by which she predicted the future. The Greek speaks literally of a "python spirit." The python was the symbol of the famous Delphic oracle and represented the god Apollo, who was believed to render predictions of future events. The serpent had thus become a symbol of augury, and anyone who was seen to possess the gift of foretelling the future was described as led by the "python." . . . So Paul, in a form reminiscent of Jesus' exorcisms, commanded the spirit to exit the girl. The spirit did so immediately.[47]

A demon empowered the girl's occult abilities, but the power of Jesus's name released her from spiritual slavery.

From the content and context of Scripture, divorcing demonic activity from the occult seems impossible. Starting in the beginning, when the serpent offered illicit supernatural knowledge to Eve, occultism has been a snare for many. But the faithful Ephesians in Acts 19:18–19 show others how to free themselves from occult practices. They burned their magical items and books, turning wholly to the Lord. The gospel of Christ and the triumph of Jesus's name outstrip the value of demonic power and knowledge.

Spiritual Warfare

From our human perspective, we use the term "spiritual warfare" to characterize the Christian struggle against evil. This warfare encompasses the detestable triad of enemies – the sinful passions that arise in fallen human nature, the ungodly patterns of a corrupt world, and the work of Satan and the demonic host. Ephesians 2:1–3 and James 4:1–7 reflect these categories

---

47. John B. Polhill, *Acts*, New American Commentary (Nashville: B & H, 1992), 351.

for understanding spiritual conflict. However when we consider the activity of demons, the phrase "spiritual warfare" refers to the skirmishes between angelic and demonic powers – combat between the spirits.

Demons war against the pure angels. In Daniel 10:13, the spiritual prince of Persia delayed an angelic ambassador to Daniel, frustrating the delivery of the answer to his prayers for a few weeks. We can even overhear a squabble between the devil and the archangel Michael in Jude 9 as they "argued about the body of Moses."[48] The apex of the biblical testimony concerning the battle between angels and demons is found in Revelation 12:7. John records, "And there was war in heaven, Michael and his angels waging war with the dragon. The dragon and his angels waged war."[49] Despite the many artistic and imaginative representations of such heavenly conflicts, the Scriptures offer scant details about this conflict. Spiritual struggles like this are still a fixture of the unseen world, but we know little about them.

Temptation

The conflict between humans and the demonic also includes temptation. After the serpent's wily deception in the garden of Eden, he and his coworkers have continued to prompt human beings to do evil. Their goal is that people may reap the holy consequences of defilement. While as James says, "each one is tempted when he is carried away and enticed by his own lust" (Jas 1:14), other evil influences and agents may encourage those lusts.[50] This understanding explains why Paul warns that Satan and his demons can exploit someone's desire to sin (1 Cor 7:5).

Christians occasionally point to how Satan tempted David to proudly assess Israel's strength through a nationwide census. First Chronicles 21:1

---

48. Schreiner asserts, "Even though the Old Testament says the Lord buried Moses (Deut 34:6), speculation arose over his burial since no human being observed the burial place. The puzzling element in Jude is the reference to the argument over the body of Moses between Michael and the devil. The terms used suggest a legal dispute over Moses' body. By establishing Moses' guilt, the devil would deprive him of the right of an honorable burial and presumably claim ownership over his body." Schreiner, *1, 2 Peter, Jude*, 458.

49. Daniel Green explains, "The second sign is a war in heaven, further accentuating the age-old battle that would continue through the tribulation period. This pitched conflict featured Michael (the leader of God's faithful angels) versus Satan (the leader of the demonic foes) (v. 7), with Michael's followers prevailing (v. 8)." Daniel Green, "Revelation," in *The Moody Bible Commentary*, ed. Michael Rydelnik and Michael Vanlaningham (Chicago: Moody, 2014), 2015.

50. According to Dibelius and Greeven, "This verse names the true source of temptations: not God, but desire!" Martin Dibelius and Heinrich Greeven, *James: A Commentary on the Epistle of James*, Hermeneia (Philadelphia: Fortress, 1976), 93.

records, "Then Satan stood up against Israel and incited David to count Israel." Thompson assumes that this text refers to the person of Satan:

> In 2 Sam 24:1 it was the Lord whose anger against Israel (the reason is not given) led him to "incite" David to count Israel. Satan is not mentioned there. At any rate, the Samuel passage suggests that the sinful designs of Satan and David were used by the Lord as agents of his wrath.[51]

But was this actually Satan – or simply "an adversary," the literal translation of the word? If we conclude that this was an attack of Satan himself, this single temptation was horrifically effective in prompting the wrathful and just punishment of God upon his disobedient people, whom David represented. By targeting a specific person, Satan was able to inflict harm throughout the Jewish nation.

But if we look more closely, the remainder of the narrative casts the angel of the Lord as the one with the drawn sword! Especially if we consider the parallel text in 2 Samuel 24 which identifies the Lord as the "inciter," Heiser's conclusion is probably correct: "This adversary [*satan*] is later identified as the angel of Yahweh in both accounts."[52] The 1 Chronicles 21 and 2 Samuel 23 incident then lines up with a similar use of *satan* in Numbers 22:22, when God confronts Balaam as an "adversary." Thus, 1 Chronicles 21:1 is not the best case for demonstrating the activity of the demonic in temptation.

However, we should expect the demonic host to trouble the church with temptation. Remember that Paul encouraged the Ephesian church to "stand firm" against "the spiritual forces of wickedness in the heavenly places" (Eph 6:11, 12).[53] When one unprepared person in the body of Christ is dragged into temptation, the consequences can disturb our witness to the community, seduce others into sin, and provoke God's discipline upon the church.

One specific avenue for the temptation of believers is sexual relationships. First Corinthians 7:5 says to married believers, "Stop depriving one another, except by agreement for a time so that you may devote yourselves to prayer, and come together again so that Satan will not tempt you because of your

---

51. J. A. Thompson, *1, 2 Chronicles*, New American Commentary (Nashville: B & H, 1994), 161.

52. Heiser, *Demons*, 80.

53. Of Eph 6:11–12 Lenski states, "Paul lets the whole army of the devil parade before our eyes. This is the tremendous power we face, against this we must stand victorious. Equipped with God's armor, we can." R. C. H. Lenski, *The Interpretation of St. Paul's Epistles to the Galatians, to the Ephesians and to the Philippians* (Minneapolis: Augsburg, 1961), 658.

lack of self-control."[54] We should not leap to the conclusion that all sexual sin is prompted by demons. But a prolonged absence of intercourse in marriage creates vulnerability which Satan can exploit for his purposes.

Of course, tempting to sexual sin is only one kind of demonic temptation of humanity. Recall the words of Paul in Ephesians 2:1–3:

> And you were dead in your offenses and sins, in which you previously walked according to the course of this world, according to the prince of the power of the air, of the spirit that is now working in the sons of disobedience. Among them we too all previously lived in the lusts of our flesh, indulging the desires of the flesh and of the mind, and were by nature children of wrath, even as the rest.[55]

When depicting the world, Paul asserts that human beings are following their desires and lusts as creatures of wrath. But the demonic powers, headed by Satan, are an integral part of this predicament, for they toil in and among us, corporately and individually, to promote evil. While Christians have freedom from these powers, we are not immune from their temptations which spread unrighteousness. After all, Satan is the "tempter."[56]

Accusation

The Greek word translated "devil" means "slanderer."[57] And Satan accuses God's people, as Scripture attests through the Old Testament accounts of Job and of

---

54. According to Dickason, "Satan promotes the philosophy of the priority of bodily satisfaction.... God has provided marriage for the normal expression of sex, and partners must recognize their mutual responsibilities. They provide Satan with an opportunity to tempt to sexual sins when there is not satisfaction in marriage." Dickason, *Angels*, 146.

55. Lincoln states,
> Paul, in 1 Cor 2:12, had recognized that there is a spirit at work in the world which is the antithesis to the Spirit of God. Here in Ephesians, that spiritual force is said to be under the rule of the same evil being who rules the air. The writer makes clear that this ruler's evil influence has both a cosmic and a human sphere.... Although the ruler of this world has been defeated cf. 1:20–22, he is not surrendering without a struggle and without still making his powerful influence felt.

Lincoln, *Ephesians*, 97.

56. 1 Thessalonians 3:5. Fee argues that Paul is explicitly tying the Thessalonians' "present hardships to satanic activity." Gordon D. Fee, *The First and Second Letters to the Thessalonians*, New International Commentary on the New Testament (Grand Rapids: Eerdmans, 2009), 119.

57. The Greek work *diabolos* (devil) "was an adjective generally denoting something or someone 'slanderous' or 'defamatory.'" G. J. Riley, "Devil," *Dictionary of Deities and Demons*, 244.

Joshua the high priest in Zechariah 3:1–2: "Then he showed me Joshua the high priest standing before the angel of the LORD, and Satan standing at his right to accuse him. And the LORD said to Satan, 'The LORD rebuke you, Satan! Indeed, the LORD who has chosen Jerusalem rebuke you! Is this not a log snatched from the fire?'" George Klein explains:

> Satan functions as the prosecutor in the trial. Satan's presence in vv. 3–4 serves as an accusation of Joshua's guilt in committing crimes against the Lord. These transgressions disqualified the priest from divine service. The setting in Zech 3 bears a striking resemblance to the heavenly courtroom in Job 1 where Satan accused Job before God.[58]

It then should be no surprise that Satan and his fallen comrades would use accusations and slander as methods of warfare against us, both in heaven and on earth, preying upon our weaknesses (1 Tim 5:14). Therefore, Revelation 12:10 refers to Satan as "the accuser of our brothers and sisters . . . the one who accuses them before our God day and night."[59]

We can also view a case of apparent accusation from the fourth chapter of Job. Eliphaz, in his ungodly opposition of Job, appeals to the whispers of a nocturnal spirit (Job 4:15–16). Alden says, "Eliphaz heard something superhuman in a quiet voice."[60] This spirit supplies information to strengthen Eliphaz's reasoning, which God ultimately rebukes. The spirit says:

> Can mankind be righteous before God?
> Can a man be pure before his Maker?
> He puts no trust even in His servants;
> And He accuses His angels of error.
> How much more those who live in houses of clay,
> Whose foundation is in the dust,
> Who are crushed before the moth! (Job 4:17–19)[61]

---

58. George L. Klein, *Zechariah*, New American Commentary (Nashville: B & H, 2007), 133.

59. Lenski states, "The names used in v. 9 point to these two designations: 'the accuser, the one accusing,' who makes it his terrible business to accuse." R. C. H. Lenski, *The Interpretation of St. John's Revelation* (Minneapolis: Augsburg, 1963), 379.

60. Alden, *Job*, 87. Job 4:15–16 says, "Then a spirit passed by my face; The hair of my flesh stood up. Something was standing still, but I could not recognize its appearance; A form was before my eyes; There was silence, then I heard a voice."

61. Mayhew states, "When Eliphaz referred to dust in v. 19, it is likely that he acquired the information to connect dust with the Maker of man and the habitation of man, not to mention the material the Maker used to create man, from Genesis (Gn 2:7). Even angels, God's servants (possibly fallen angels and Satan), are not perfect, so certainly humans are perishable and die,

This spirit belittles the standing of human beings before God, similar to Satan's heavenly questioning of Job in the preceding chapters. Muddling truth with accusation, this deceitful demon even raises the issue of how God judges sinful angels. How much more should frail humans be subject to God's wrath, so to speak? The accusing spirit raises a perspective that leaves no room for redemption or vindication, two concepts that the demonic host never experience in the biblical record, which are what Job eventually receives. This accusation, along with the human agent who delivered it, fails.

Inhabitation[62]

Many a curious student of the Scriptures has lingered over demon inhabitation, but the Bible does not. The Old Testament includes only a handful of descriptions of demonic inhabitation, and no formal exorcisms (e.g. 1 Sam 18:10, perhaps 1 Kgs 22:21–23). The New Testament includes some exorcism narratives, but none outside of the Synoptic Gospels (Matthew, Mark, and Luke) and Acts. The conclusion is straightforward: The Bible does not elevate demonization as the chief activity of demons. Consequently, the church's chief activity is not exorcism. We do poorly if our churches and ministries are on one hand unable to deal with a demon or on the other hand obsessed with casting out spirits.[63] Rather, we can follow the model of Christ and the apostles who occasionally performed exorcisms as a part of missional outreach focused on preaching. In Acts 16, Paul did not enter Philippi to perform exorcisms, though he did perform one after a couple of days! His priority was to proclaim the gospel.

While not a focal point, demonization is an obvious type of demonic activity in Scripture. One prolonged case is described in Mark 9.

> And one person from the crowd answered Him, "Teacher, I brought You my son, because he has a spirit that makes him unable

---

yet without wisdom." Eugene J. Mayhew, "Job," in *The Moody Bible Commentary*, ed. Michael Rydelnik and Michael Vanlaningham (Chicago: Moody, 2014), 708.

62. In this work, "inhabitation" and "demonization" are used in place of the common term "demon possession." While "demon possessed" is used in some English translations of the New Testament, the translation of the Greek δαιμονίζομαι or ἔχω does not require the latter portion "possessed." While conveying the same idea of inhabitation, using a term other than "demon possession" assists us in avoiding any confusion or connotation that demons possess or own human bodies. No translation effort is perfect but "inhabitation" and "demonization" are more suitable.

63. We should find it odd that no exorcisms occur in a church service in the biblical record, though this practice is popular throughout the world today.

to speak; and whenever it seizes him, it slams him to the ground, and he foams at the mouth and grinds his teeth and becomes stiff. And I told Your disciples so that they would cast it out, but they could not do it." . . .

And they brought the boy to Him. When he saw Him, the spirit immediately threw him into convulsions, and falling to the ground, he began rolling around and foaming at the mouth. And He asked his father, "How long has this been happening to him?" And he said, "From childhood. It has often thrown him both into the fire and into the water to kill him. But if You can do anything, take pity on us and help us!". . .

When Jesus saw that a crowd was rapidly gathering, He rebuked the unclean spirit, saying to it, "You deaf and mute spirit, I command you, come out of him and do not enter him again." And after crying out and throwing him into terrible convulsions, it came out; and the boy became so much like a corpse that most of them said, "He is dead!" But Jesus took him by the hand and raised him; and he got up. (Mark 9:17–18, 20–22, 25–27)

Not only was this demon inhabiting and occasionally controlling the child, but it was violent and destructive. Evans says, "The grim summary of what this evil spirit has done to the boy clarifies the desperation felt by the father. The demonic possession is not only disruptive and oppressive but dangerous and potentially fatal."[64] The demon had nearly killed the child and was responsible for the physical symptoms of muteness and deafness.

In the biblical portrayals of demonization, the text does not scientifically and thoroughly analyze the symptoms or pathways to inhabitation. Having that expectation of Scripture is evidence of the Western cultural thinking of academic evaluation and skepticism. But the biblical narratives do provide some details. Symptoms vary widely, from the painful and self-destructive behavior of the Gerasene demoniac to the partnership with the fortune-telling slave girl discussed above. Many people who are demonized are also described as having some vulnerability, including being young like the boy above who was inhabited since childhood and the daughter of the Canaanite woman (Matt 15:22–28); having sinful tendencies like the greed of Judas prior to Satan inhabiting him (John 12:6); having a relationship to occultism or false worship like the Philippian slave girl (Acts 16:16); or being subject to divine

---

64. Evans, *Mark 8:27–16:20*, 52.

judgment like Saul (1 Sam 18:10). These biblical descriptions give us general pathways to inhabitation, and the specifics are numerous around the world since each culture usually has historically recognized pathways for voluntary and involuntary inhabitation.

We should also mention that the Bible does not outright portray inhabitation as a threat against the church. Because of our status as God's children and the residence of the Holy Spirit within us, many believers argue that we are sheltered from complete inhabitation or "possession" on the level of the raving demoniac of Mark 5, even though we can experience demonic influence, bullying, harassment, and affliction. Christians can be oppressed, but not possessed.[65] However, some do believe that Christians indwelt by the Holy Spirit can also be inhabited by a demon, though the symptoms are more mild.

The debate involves the use of the words "possessed" and "oppressed," along with accompanying systems of thought. While a true Christian is certainly "possessed" by God through the redeeming work of Christ and not possessed by an evil spirit, to what level can Christians be affected or inhabited? Arguing for the possibility of Christians experiencing demonization, Karl Payne shares the need for nuance.

> The problem is that the simplicity of the either/or paradigm [possessed or oppressed] doesn't fully account for Bible verses that allow for the demonization of Christians. It also doesn't account for the testimonies of Christian laymen and leaders in North America and around the world whose struggles certainly appear more severe than oppression but that fall short of total demonic control and domination.[66]

While the debate will inevitably continue, a concrete consensus arises around the fact that Christians have special advantages and resources in conflicts with the demonic because of God's gracious salvation through Jesus, the Messiah. In summary, demonization is described in the Bible as one of many activities of beings in the demonic realm. Inhabitation is one vehicle

---

65. The English term "oppression," as it is used by the NASB translators, seems to be of broader meaning in the Bible. This is reflected in Acts 10:38 where it says Jesus healed "all who were oppressed by the devil." Considering the New Testament occasionally refers to exorcisms as healings (e.g. Luke 9:42), the statement is probably broad, including exorcisms of the inhabited. In that light, it can prove difficult to utilize the "Christians can be oppressed but not possessed" paradigm when texts like this one exist. Those who assert that a Christian cannot be inhabited by a demon could employ a better term like "harassed."

66. Karl Payne, *Spiritual Warfare: Christians, Demonization, and Deliverance* (Washington, DC: WND, 2011), 171.

they use to afflict, deceive, tempt, accuse, and torment human beings. It is a demonic activity yet also a conduit for their operations.

Affliction

As we have reflected on the story of the demonized son in Mark 9, we find that the portrayal of demons causing human suffering challenges us. This theme is a thread that runs through the Scriptures from the beginning. Deceiving humanity leads to suffering and pain.

The book of Job presents probably the most obvious biblical example of human suffering originating from evil powers. The narrative reads:

> Then the LORD said to Satan, "Behold, all that he [Job] has is in your power, only do not reach out and put your hand on him." So Satan departed from the presence of the LORD.
>
> Now on the day when his sons and his daughters were eating and drinking wine in their oldest brother's house, a messenger came to Job and said, "The oxen were plowing and the female donkeys feeding beside them, and the Sabeans attacked and took them. They also killed the servants with the edge of the sword, and I alone have escaped to tell you." While he was still speaking, another came and said, "The fire of God fell from heaven and burned up the sheep and the servants and consumed them, and I alone have escaped to tell you." While he was still speaking, another came and said, "The Chaldeans formed three units and made a raid on the camels and took them, and killed the servants with the edge of the sword, and I alone have escaped to tell you." While he was still speaking, another also came and said, "Your sons and your daughters were eating and drinking wine in their oldest brother's house, and behold, a great wind came from across the wilderness and struck the four corners of the house, and it fell on the young people and they died, and I alone have escaped to tell you."...
>
> Then Satan went out from the presence of the LORD and struck Job with severe boils from the sole of his foot to the top of his head. (Job 1:12–19; 2:7)[67]

---

67. Hartley observes,
    These four plagues revealed to Job that all the forces of heaven and earth had turned hostile toward him. This idea is borne out by the fact that the causes of destruction alternate between earthly and heavenly forces coming from all four

God grants Satan a remarkable and terrifying amount of latitude in this divinely orchestrated test of Job.[68] Consider all that is under the power of Satan!

1. The attacks of the Sabeans and the Chaldeans
2. The lives of servants and children
3. The loss of wealth (animals)
4. The fire from heaven
5. The wind from the wilderness
6. The health of Job

This catastrophic affliction originated from satanic power. Yet Job was unmoved, and he recognized God's supremacy by acknowledging that he ultimately gives and takes away.

As seen in prior texts, affliction is occasionally associated with the demonic activity of demonization. But some cases of affliction are more ambiguous. Luke the physician records the following:

> And there was a woman who for eighteen years had had a sickness caused by a spirit; and she was bent double, and could not straighten up at all. When Jesus saw her, He called her over and said to her, "Woman, you are freed from your sickness." And He laid His hands on her; and immediately she stood up straight again and began glorifying God. (Luke 13:11–13)[69]

---

points of the compass: the Sabeans from the south, lightning from a storm out of the west, the Chaldeans from the north, and the treacherous sirocco blowing off the desert to the east. The number four also symbolizes full measure, totality. John E. Hartley, *The Book of Job*, New International Commentary on the Old Testament (Grand Rapids: Eerdmans, 1988), 77.

68. The Hebrew text literally reads "the satan," referring to role of accuser rather than giving a person's name. But because of the remainder of the canon, we can identify "the satan" with the person of Satan in this instance.

69. Marshall states, "Certainly the illness is attributed ultimately to the evil power of Satan, but the cure is not described as an exorcism, but as a release from a fairly literal 'bond.' Perhaps we should not try to give too definite a meaning to πνεῦμα and think of it simply as an evil influence." I. Howard Marshall, *The Gospel of Luke: A Commentary on the Greek Text*, New International Greek Testament Commentary (Grand Rapids: Eerdmans, 1978), 557. Marshall is reluctant to acknowledge the possibility that an actual demon caused this condition, even though the context shares that Satan bound the woman in the malady.

Luke describes the event as a healing, even though the credit for the condition falls upon a spirit.[70] While we need not hastily conclude that a demon inhabited the woman to cause the infirmity, we are assured of the role of a fallen supernatural agent. The narrative supplies no explanation for the affliction other than that the spirit caused the woman harm.

However, the relationship of Satan and demons to human suffering and affliction in no way means that they are solely responsible for every illness and trouble faced on earth. The curse of God in Genesis 3, the brokenness of creation, the sinful nature of human beings, the corrupt patterns of cultures and families – these account for much of our experience with suffering. In most of the healing passages, the Bible does not credit demons with our afflictions. God's people should follow suit.

Defeat

Do the demonic powers battle against God? While an affirmative answer is a given, some nuance is necessary. The conflict between God and the demonic host is not necessarily an open war in many biblical texts. But they are in conflict, and the outcomes of their battles are resoundingly one-sided. Satan and the demons lose. The defeat of the demonic is a theme that saturates the biblical narrative. At nearly every turn, they encounter defeat and failure, which serve as repeated reminders of their approaching doom.

Concerning this theme of satanic defeat, we will consider a text that requires individual focus: Ezekiel 28:11–19.[71] In the list of prophetic judgments about the rulers of various nations, the prophet mentions a "king of Tyre." But the prophetic judgment against this "king" includes a description that surpasses a mere human ruler. The paragraph in question introduces a person described as a created cherub (vv. 13–14) who blamelessly lived in the garden of God, bedecked with jewels like a priest (vv. 13, 15). Who is the text discussing? After dismissing unsatisfactory explanations, Cooper suggests the following:

---

70. In Matthew 15:22–28, a case of demonization also ends in a healing when the daughter of a Canaanite woman receives the work of Christ from afar. The overlap of demonization and affliction is evident, and with the intensity of suffering experienced in demonic inhabitation, exorcism sometimes manifests as healing.

71. Isa 14:12–17 is a sister passage to Ezek 28:11–19. Cooper asserts, "Of the twenty elements associated with the king of Tyre in 28:11–19 most also are found in Isaiah's indictment of another tyrannical ruler, the king of Babylon (14:12–17)." Lamar Eugene Cooper, *Ezekiel*, New American Commentary (Nashville: B & H, 1994), 268–69. Since Ezekiel is the more substantial of the two, it will feature in this discussion of demonic defeat. Heiser in *Demons* extensively correlates Gen 3, Isa 14, and Ezek 28. See 65–70.

Who, then, was the person whose character was like the king of Tyre that fulfilled the elements of vv. 12–17? The serpent was known for his craftiness (Gen 3:1), his deceit, and his anti-God attitude (3:4), leading humanity to sin (3:6–7). Elsewhere he is presented as a deceiver (Rev 12:9; 20:2), an instigator of evil (John 13:2, 27), one who seeks worship as a god (Luke 4:6–8; 2 Thess 2:3–4), and one who seeks to get others to renounce God (Job 2:4–5). He appears as an angel of God (2 Cor 11:14) and as the father of lies and violence (John 8:44), distorts Scripture (Matt 4:6), opposes believers (2 Cor 2:11), and finally is judged (Matt 25:41; Rev 19:20–21; 20:13–15). Therefore the conclusion that the figure behind the poetic symbol is the serpent (also known as the adversary, the devil, Satan; Rev 12:9) is a logical one.[72]

Ezekiel was addressing the person who stands behind the wickedness of the nations. "The real motivating force behind the King of Tyre was the adversary . . . who opposed God and His people from the beginning."[73] He was initially a cherub, but he plunged into prideful sin. Yet this being of position and power, whom we identify as Satan, was branded by defeat from the outset of his rebellion. He was driven out in disgrace (Ezek 28:16) and cast to the earth (v. 17). In the words of Lutzer, Satan's insurrection was "a roll of the dice," and "his future was gambled in a slot machine that paid no dividends."[74] He lost, and he would keep losing.

The Bible describes the defeat of the demonic in many chapters, gradually unfolding from the fall (Gen 3). The forces of evil triumphed in the garden. But God cursed the snake and proclaimed its ultimate defeat, by human seed no less! Then a restorative flood countered the demonic and sinful corruption of humanity described in Genesis 6. Satan also accused both Job and Joshua the high priest, but to no avail.

The defeats escalated with the arrival of the incarnate Son. Jesus overcame the temptations of Satan in the wilderness with the word of God (Matt 4:1–11).[75] Without appealing to another authority, Jesus cast out demons. But Christ's battle with the enemy was not solely with biblical exegesis and exorcisms. He

---

72. Cooper, *Ezekiel*, 268.
73. Cooper, 269.
74. Lutzer, *God's Devil*, 34.
75. Hagner states, "Satan has tested Jesus and has failed. Jesus sends him away with a command that calls attention simultaneously to his victory and to his authority." Donald A. Hagner, *Matthew 1–13* (Dallas: Word, 1993), 68–69.

came with a greater salvation purpose. "The one who practices sin is of the devil; for the devil has sinned from the beginning. The Son of God appeared for this purpose, to destroy the works of the devil" (1 John 3:8).[76]

How did Jesus defeat Satan so completely? Jesus himself states the following in John 12:31–32, "Now judgment is upon this world; now the ruler of this world will be cast out. And I, if I am lifted up from the earth, will draw all people to Myself." What a picture! Beasley-Murray comments, "The utterance of Jesus employs a well-understood picture to show the change of situation for the world when Jesus was 'lifted up' to heaven via the cross: Satan was *dethroned* and the Son of Man *enthroned* over the world for which he died."[77] The death of Christ defeated Satan. The author of Hebrews explains, "Therefore, since the children share in flesh and blood, He Himself likewise also partook of the same, so that through death He might destroy the one who has the power of death, that is, the devil, and free those who through fear of death were subject to slavery all their lives" (Heb 2:14–15).[78] The cross shatters Satan's tyranny over this world filled with fear, sin, and death.

The death of Christ won freedom from the devil's purposes for sin, guilt, condemnation, and death. Christ's victory broke the power of Satan, along with his demonic viceroys, and the nations began to receive the gospel of freedom from death and its master. Jesus dispatched servants like Paul, commissioning them to reach the world, "to open their eyes so that they turn from darkness to light, and from the power of Satan to God, that they may receive forgiveness of sins and an inheritance among those who have been sanctified by faith in

---

76. Strecker and Attridge say, "To the activity of the devil, which permeates the whole course of history and causes sin, is opposed the revelation of the Son of God. . . . The purpose of [the Son of God's] appearance in history is the destruction of the works of the devil." Georg Strecker and Harold W. Attridge, *The Johannine Letters: A Commentary on 1, 2, and 3 John*, Hermeneia (Minneapolis: Fortress, 1996), 101.

77. Beasley-Murray, *John*, 213–14. Emphasis original.

78. Attridge and Koester explain,

> Christ's participation in "blood and flesh" resulted in his death, whereby he achieved a decisive victory over and "destroyed the power" . . . of the one who held sway over death. The imagery evokes the depiction of the Messiah's victory over demonic forces widespread in Jewish apocalyptic tradition and in early Christianity. This general tradition frequently becomes specified as a victory over death in Christian sources. The explicit linking of the devil and death here is also based on traditional association of Satan and death.

Harold W. Attridge and Helmut Koester, *The Epistle to the Hebrews: A Commentary on the Epistle to the Hebrews*. Hermeneia (Philadelphia: Fortress, 1989), 93.

Me" (Acts 26:18).[79] Christ's presence disturbed the old order, and he defeated it by his sacrificial mission as he unmasked and "disarmed the rulers and authorities" (Col 2:15).[80] Cowering before him, the forces of wickedness lost when Christ arrived.

With Christ's arrival, ministry, and departure, his followers began to share in his victory over the demonic, but not without effort and struggle. Luke 9:37–43 describes how the disciples were frustrated by a demon; yet seventy-two of them prevailed over demons according to Luke 10:17–20! But by trusting in the power and authority of Jesus, Christians are described in Acts as putting demons to flight. The story of Philip was one prominent example.

> Philip went down to the city of Samaria and began proclaiming Christ to them. The crowds were paying attention with one mind to what was being said by Philip, as they heard and saw the signs which he was performing. For in the case of many who had unclean spirits, they were coming out of them shouting with a loud voice; and many who had been paralyzed or limped on crutches were healed. So there was much rejoicing in that city. (Acts 8:5–8)[81]

In the midst of triumphs, the early Christian church was not immune from setbacks: Satan filled the hearts of Ananias and Sapphira, perhaps aiming

---

79. Polhill states,

> Ultimately, the role of witness is the key role for every disciple. All who have encountered the risen Christ are commissioned to be witnesses (Acts 1:8). . . . Christ is the servant of God who opens the eyes of those in darkness, who brings light to the nations. To proclaim him is to bring the light of the gospel. It could hardly be more aptly summarized than Paul did here. The gospel brings light, opens one's eyes to the truth in Christ. Paul further described this as a turning from the power of Satan to the power of God. The sharp dualistic language of light and darkness is found throughout the New Testament and is metaphorical for two divergent ways of living. The one way can be described in various ways – living according to the world, under Satan, in darkness, in sin, apart from God, totally self-centered existence. The alternative is life in Christ, a life marked by righteousness, walking in the light, directed by God and not by self.

Polhill, *Acts*, 504.

80. Melick states, "A paradox occurred. Jesus hung naked and disgraced, dying publicly for sinners. The evil forces assumed they had triumphed. In reality, through this act of both sacrifice and triumph, God disgraced these evil beings. The tables were turned. God triumphed in the redemptive work of Christ." Richard R. Melick, *Philippians, Colossians, Philemon*, New American Commentary (Nashville: B & H, 1991), 266.

81. Polhill states, "Philip's preaching, like that of the Jerusalem apostles, was undergirded by 'signs,' miracles that pointed beyond themselves to the power and life to be found in the one he proclaimed (v. 6). Demons were exorcised. Paralytics and lame persons were healed (v. 7). Ultimately, it was the gospel they responded to, not the miracles (v. 12)." Polhill, *Acts*, 215.

to corrupt the church in its infancy (Acts 5:3).[82] But the spiritual armor that Paul describes in Ephesians 6 reminds Christians that they have been supplied every resource necessary to thrive in battle with the enemy and his demonic horde. James encourages believers in Jesus to, "Submit therefore to God. Resist the devil and he will flee from you" (Jas 4:7).[83] The defeats continue as do the so-called victories, such as when a messenger (or angel) from Satan afflicted Paul (2 Cor 12:7). Yet God redirects even these small satanic victories for his purposes and the good of his people.[84]

Greater defeats yet loom ahead for the demonic powers. According to Revelation 20, Satan will be bound in the abyss for the millennial period, prior to his demise in the lake of fire.

> Then I saw an angel coming down from heaven, holding the key of the abyss and a great chain in his hand. And he laid hold of the dragon, the serpent of old, who is the devil and Satan, and bound him for a thousand years; and he threw him into the abyss and shut it and sealed it over him, so that he would not deceive the nations any longer, until the thousand years were completed; after these things he must be released for a short time. . . .
>
> And the devil who deceived [the nations] was thrown into the lake of fire and brimstone, where the beast and the false prophet

---

82. Polhill explains, "All this had happened because he had allowed the archenemy of the Spirit, Satan, to enter his heart. Satan 'filled' Ananias's heart just as he had Judas's (cf. Luke 22:3). Like Judas, Ananias was motivated by money (cf. Luke 22:5). But in filling the heart of one of its members, Satan had now entered for the first time into the young Christian community as well." Polhill, 158.

83. Richardson states,
> The next admonition of this verse calls the believer to put up active resistance to the devil and his influence. Although humbling oneself does not cause the devil to flee, such submission to God is an important precondition for doing battle with the devil. But a defensive posture is all that is required to rout the evil one: resist him, and he will flee. . . . if he is consciously resisted, in submission to God, the devil cannot fight back and must flee the attack that is our resistance to him.

Kurt A. Richardson, *James*, New American Commentary (Nashville: B & H, 1997), 185.

84. Garland asks,
> Does this satanic angel try to hinder the advance of the gospel in some way (see 1 Thess 2:18)? If so, Satan's purposes are thwarted (see 2:11). What is sent to torment Paul is transformed by God into a means of proclaiming Christ's power and grace. This surprising twist reflects the paradoxical way God defeats Satan. God permits Satan to strike the apostle, but God turns the stricken Paul into an even greater instrument of his power.

Garland, *2 Corinthians*, 522.

are also; and they will be tormented day and night forever and ever. (Rev 20:1–3, 10)[85]

All of Satan's rebellious efforts will culminate after the millennium, yet the Lord and his saints will prevail. As Paul declares in the book of Romans, alluding to the curse of the serpent in Genesis 3, "The God of peace will soon crush Satan under your feet" (Rom 16:20).[86] Total defeat of the devil is near. This downfall will be a fitting conclusion to Satan's long but fruitless rebellion, and his coworkers will not receive exemption. God will punish the entire demonic realm! Isaiah prophesied the following:

> So it will happen in that day,
> That the LORD will punish the rebellious angels of heaven on high,
> And the kings of the earth on earth.
> They will be gathered together
> Like prisoners in the dungeon,
> And will be confined in prison;
> And after many days they will be punished. (Isa 24:21–22)[87]

---

85. Green explains,

> The abyss is a place of confinement for certain demons prior to their eternal torment in the lake of fire. Satan would be bound there for a thousand years to keep him from deceiving the nations during the reign of Christ.... Not even experiencing the wonderful leadership of Christ and the ideal environment of the millennium will convince these insurgents [the people who follow Satan after his release from the abyss] to obey. After this, the devil ... will be cast into the lake of fire to join the beast and the false prophet.

Green, "Revelation," 2024.

86. Jewett and Kotansky explain, "The metaphor of crushing a foe underfoot evokes martial victory both in the Hebrew and in the Greco-Roman traditions. The familiar refrains from Ps 110 of making enemies a 'footstool' and Ps 8 of placing all things 'under his feet' echo through the NT. Ps 91:13 promises that with God's assistance, the elect will tread on dangerous serpents and wild beasts, fulfilling the promise of Gen 3:15." Robert K. Jewett and Roy D. Kotansky, *Romans: A Commentary*, Hermeneia (Minneapolis: Fortress, 2007), 994. But how will Christians be involved in crushing Satan? Paul in 1 Cor 6:3 hints when he says, "Do you not know that we will judge angels?" Conzelmann states, "In Christianity the office of judge is transferred also to Christ. And thus those who are 'in Christ' also have part in it.... [1 Cor 6:3] is couched in parallel terms and expands the idea to include even angels." Conzelmann, *1 Corinthians*, 105.

87. Smith explains,

> The defiled natural, inanimate world will feel the brunt of God's wrath, but so will all living creatures, especially those powers in heaven and earth that oppose God. Once these are defeated "in that day," God's final and victorious reign will be fully established. The purpose of God's final visitation will be to bring low the powers on earth (24:21, 22) and in the heavens (24:21, 23), leaving God himself as the reigning king (24:23b).... The heavenly hosts could refer to the stars and planets (40:26; 45:12; Ps 33:6), but it seems more likely that this is a reference to enemy angelic beings (2 Kings 22:19; Job 1:6; Dan 4:32; 8:10; 10:13),

For Christ to reign directly on the earth, he must defeat every opponent to the true God, including the kings of the nations with their arrogance and the demons with their deceit.

"Have You come here to torment us before the time?" (Matt 8:29). When the demons encountered Jesus, this cry reflected their terror.[88] Soon, the time they fear will arrive, and their defeat will be complete. Their activity will cease, and they will become everlasting recipients of God's holy wrath. As Jesus said, Satan and his angels will enter the judgment prepared for them.[89]

---

not inanimate objects. The parallelism between the two halves of this verse invites the comparison between the defeat of the powerful evil rulers on earth (21b) and the powerful rulers in heaven (21a). Once these are defeated God alone will rule the world.

Gary V. Smith, *Isaiah 1–39*, New American Commentary (Nashville: B & H, 2007), 424.

88. According to Hagner, "The demons' subsequent question . . . is interesting from at least two respects: first, in it the demons recognize that at the eschatological judgment they will experience God's judgment and the end of their power . . . and second, they recognize that [the time] has not yet come; Jesus has in effect come too early and threatens their realm too soon." Hagner, *Matthew 1–13*, 227.

89. "Then He will also say to those on His left, 'Depart from Me, you accursed people, into the eternal fire which has been prepared for the devil and his angels" (Matt 25:41). Lenski states, "Hell fire was originally prepared for the devil and his angels as the fit punishment for their irremediable apostasy from God." R. C. H. Lenski, *The Interpretation of St. Matthew's Gospel* (Minneapolis: Augsburg, 1961), 997.

5

The Recorded Speech of Demons

Divine revelatory literature is selective. If you read aloud Matthew 5–7, the Sermon on the Mount, it is not much longer than ten minutes. The passage is a short (i.e. shortened) sermon! The apostle John openly admits that his gospel is limited in scope: "But there are also many other things which Jesus did, which if they were written in detail, I expect that even the world itself would not contain the books that would be written" (John 21:25).[1] Setting aside the secondary events, the essence of the mission of Christ is front and center.

The Twelve Demonic Speeches

The Scriptures also do not detail every exorcism or every conversation with a demon. Since the Bible is about God, his purposes for self-revelation, and the redemption of humanity, the spirits are not central characters. Scriptural references to exorcisms are sometimes presented in passing without elaboration (Luke 10:17–20; Acts 8:7). Even more, demonic speech is rare in the canon, especially in comparison to the volumes of human and divine discourse. Demons say little in all the biblical accounts. Jesus silences them (Mark 1:34), and the Holy Spirit quiets them through his oversight of the Bible's composition. These facts mean that when a biblical passage does include demonic speech, the sentences are important. In tandem with our analysis of ten demonic activities, let us now examine twelve demonic utterances.

---

1. According to Keener, "When writers had more data before them than they could record, they often noted that they were being selective. . . . Greek, Jewish and Samaritan writers often included hyperboles like this one as well, sometimes speaking of how the world could not contain the knowledge a particular rabbi had of the law, and so forth." Craig S. Keener, *The IVP Bible Background Commentary: New Testament* (Downers Grove: InterVarsity, 2014), 313.

The Arrogant Gambler

> But you said in your heart,
> **"I will ascend to heaven;**
> **I will raise my throne above the stars of God,**
> **And I will sit on the mount of assembly**
> **In the recesses of the north.**
> **I will ascend above the heights of the clouds;**
> **I will make myself like the Most High."** (Isa 14:13–14)

Is this demonic, satanic speech? Like Ezekiel 28, Isaiah 14:4 mentions an earthly king, "king of Babylon." Even with that designation, Oswalt admits, "there is no indication that he [Isaiah] has one particular person [the king] in mind."[2] Though a few advocate for some satanic dimension to this text, many modern commentators like Oswalt are resolute in their rejection that this text refers or alludes to the satanic rebellion.[3] Certainly, one's hermeneutic of prophetic, poetic literature is tested. Is the genre fluid enough to permit subject changes and historical allusions in the middle of a passage describing a human ruler? Probably so.

However, the denial that Isaiah 14:13–14 is the thoughts of Satan stands in stark contrast to the overwhelming testimony of the church fathers which acknowledges that these verses allude to Satan. An example from Augustine of Hippo demonstrates this historical perspective.

> How, then, did the devil seize what did not belong to him? "I will set my throne in the north; I shall be like the Most High," he said. He grabbed for himself something not given to him; that was robbery. The devil tried to usurp what had not been granted to him and thereby lost what he had been given. Then from the cup of his own pride he offered a drink to the humans he was trying to seduce, saying, "Taste it, and you will be like gods." They too wanted to make a grab at divinity, and they lost their happiness.[4]

---

2. John Oswalt, *The Book of Isaiah, Chapters 1–39*, New International Commentary on the Old Testament (Grand Rapids: Eerdmans, 1986), 314.

3. See Cooper's analysis of Ezekiel 28, which includes its relationship to Isaiah 14, in the New American Commentary series for a modern proponent who defends this text as a reference to Satan.

4. Augustine of Hippo, *Explanations of the Psalms 68*, quoted in Steven A. McKinion, ed., *Isaiah 1–39*, Ancient Christian Commentary Series 10 (Downers Grove, IL: InterVarsity, 2004), 124.

Despite the interpretive divide between pre- and post-Reformation scholars, the connection between Isaiah 14 and the rebellion of Satan seems too obvious to ignore. Yes, earthly kings are in view in Isaiah 14 and Ezekiel 28. But Heiser summarizes these chapters and then states, "Some scholars . . . believe that, while each prophetic taunt/lament is directed at a human king, both passages draw on a primeval tale of a *divine* [satanic] rebellion to portray the respective kings the way they do."[5]

Even if we do not think that Isaiah prophesied with Satan in mind, Augustine shows us a way forward together. Whether human kings or demonic powers utter these words, they still represent all rebellion against God – in the garden or even by angels. Created beings wish to reign in the place of God.

Imagine what it would have been like to be the first creature to rebel against God! You would have never seen the justice of God. Your action would have been the wildest arrogant leap, a celestial gamble with unused dice. Little would you know that your lust for power and freedom would only win you wrath and bondage.

The Serpent in the Garden

> Now the serpent was more cunning than any animal of the field which the LORD God had made. And he said to the woman, **"Has God really said, 'You shall not eat from any tree of the garden?'"** . . . **"You surely will not die! For God knows that in the day you eat from it your eyes will be opened, and you will become like God, knowing good and evil."** (Gen 3:1, 4–5)

Again, questions persist as to whether this section is satanic speech. If we were studying Genesis 1–3 in seclusion, away from the canon of Scripture and the tradition of God's people throughout history, one could understand the skepticism. Mathews answers the critics.

> Many modern interpreters, however, fail to recognize that the serpent's trickery is ultimately the voice of Satan. Although the snake is never identified as Satan in the Old Testament, more than the principle of evil must have been intended by the serpent's presence since 3:15 describes an ongoing war between the serpent and the seed of the woman. "All the days of your life" (3:14) shows that the serpent is treated as a personal being. . . . In accord with

---

5. Heiser, *Demons*, 67, italics original.

the traditional opinion, the snake is more than a literal snake; rather it is Satan's personal presence in the garden.[6]

Unless we toss out the context and the remainder of the scriptural testimony, we must recognize that a supernatural being is manipulating God's good creation for decidedly evil ends that embody the demonic rebellion against God.

Many books address the fall of humanity. Christians reflect on Genesis 3 at length. But when we separate the serpent's words from the chapter-long dialogue, it produces shock. Is that all the serpent said? Of course, selection is probably in play, for the temptation may have taken some length of time. Yet the Scriptures by the inspiration of the Holy Spirit barely record a paragraph of speech from the old serpent, "the great dragon" – the leader of the rebellious angels (Rev 12:7-9).

The serpent's efforts intertwine deception and temptation. His initial line forces Eve into mounting a defense of God and his law. This dialogue leads to questions concerning God's character. The translation of the Hebrew statement as a question is a touch problematic, with Victor Hamilton suggesting that it is a "feigned expression of surprise."[7] Hamilton explains the serpent's first sentence.

> [The serpent] grossly exaggerates God's prohibition, claiming that God did not allow them access to any of the orchard trees. Apart from this claim being unadulterated distortion, it is an attempt to create in the woman's mind the impression that God is spiteful, mean, obsessively jealous, and self-protective. In addition, it cleverly provides Eve with an opportunity to defend God and to clarify his position, for by this one statement of the snake God has moved from beneficent provider to cruel oppressor.[8]

This tactic cunningly prepares Eve for the thrust of the serpent's argument, that God is not right, true, or good in preventing human beings from being "like God." The doubt about God and the desire to eat festers in the heart of Eve. At that moment, human beings begin to dictate to God what they deemed to be good, in contrast to what the Creator God declares to be good.

What did the serpent mean when he said, "like God" or "like *elohim*" in Genesis 3:5? While most English translations render the Hebrew *elohim* as

---

6. Mathews, *Genesis 1–11:26*, 234.

7. Victor P. Hamilton, *The Book of Genesis, Chapters 1–17*, New International Commentary on the Old Testament (Grand Rapids: Eerdmans, 1990), 191. He renders the phrase as, "Indeed! To think that God said you are not to eat of any tree of the garden!" 186.

8. Hamilton, *Book of Genesis*, 189.

"God," the word can also refer to "gods," since this word for God is the plural of "god." Furthermore, coming from the mouth of a supernatural serpent, it is possible that he is suggesting that Eve could be like the gods, the angelic powers, who know good and evil. As Heiser argues, the key to this argument rests in Genesis 3:22, where God asserts that human beings have "become like one of Us, knowing good and evil." Heiser says, "This means that the *elohim* of verse 5 points to a group – God's heavenly council."[9] Diverging from Heiser, who advocates that the serpent alone had fallen at this point and that other angels joined his rebellion closer to the flood, this statement could lead us to assume that some angels had already rebelled, and the council that served the Lord included powers both good and evil.[10]

Let us return to what we know with more confidence. With her human heart vulnerable through the serpent's initial tactic, the satanic strike fell upon Eve with devastating force. The Deceiver exploited the first couple's innocence.

> The serpent made three counterclaims: First, they will not die. Second, "your eyes will be opened," a metaphor for knowledge, suggesting a newfound awareness not previously possessed. . . . And finally, they will gain what belongs to God, "knowing good and evil." Essentially he is contending that God is holding her back – a claim that is sometimes echoed today.[11]

In these three assertions, we observe the deception and temptation that the demons use. While schemes and contexts change, the lies of deathlessness,

---

9. Heiser, *Demons*, 64.

10. Did the serpent rebel alone? Avoiding any notion of the existence of an early rebel faction, Heiser states, "For being the first divine rebel, the villain of Eden would become perceived as 'the god of this world' (2 Cor 4:4)." Heiser, 81. This rebel is the first and lonely "defector." Heiser, 83. At first blush, this idea is plausible, but it certainly seems like poor strategy to mount an attack on God via his creation with no alliance in the divine council. In total, Heiser argues for three rebellions against God by the heavenly host: in the garden of Eden, before the flood, and in the building of the tower of Babel. Heiser is pushing back against church tradition, but what if the tradition makes the most sense, biblically speaking? We know that Satan swept a third of the "stars" (angels) out of heaven (Rev 12:4), perhaps during the incarnation, but who is to say that they were not previously corrupt in heaven? Also, God created hell for the devil and his angels (Matt 25:41). Why would we assume that this creation was long after Satan's initial deception in the garden? The overall thread of Scripture does not overtly point us toward successive rebellions. It may perhaps lean toward something like the traditional view, though we need not think Satan and his host left heaven in the beginning, with new demonic schemes in history and God's heightened punishments in response. What Heiser calls independent rebellions, we can call skirmishes that follow from the initial drawing of battle lines in the heavenly places.

11. Mathews, *Genesis 1–11:26*, 237.

hidden knowledge, and humans becoming like gods abound in the rebellious systems of every age.

The Accuser of Job in the Heavens

> The LORD said to Satan, "From where do you come?" Satan answered the LORD and said, "**From roaming about on the earth and walking around on it.**" ... Then Satan answered the LORD, "**Does Job fear God for nothing? Have You not made a fence around him and his house and all that he has, on every side? You have blessed the work of his hands, and his possessions have increased in the land. But reach out Your hand now and touch all that he has; he will surely curse You to Your face.**" (Job 1:7, 9–11)
>
> The LORD said to Satan, "Where have you come from?" Then Satan answered the LORD and said, "**From roaming about on the earth and walking around on it.**" ... Satan answered the LORD and said, "**Skin for skin! Yes, all that a man has, he will give for his life. However, reach out Your hand now, and touch his bone and his flesh; he will curse You to Your face!**" (Job 2:2, 4–5)

We seldom experience the privilege of peering into the third heaven – the abode of God. The beginning of Job ushers us into the assembly of the holy ones, the sons of God. During this grand presentation, the accuser (Satan) appears. This scene repeats in Job 1 and 2, and twice the Lord initiates a conversation with Satan about Job. While "accuser" bears the connotation of a legal role in prosecuting the wicked, Satan instead functions "as a troublemaker, a disturber of the kingdom."[12] The heavens are not as peaceful as we might envision them!

Is this actually Satan? Or is this being in the heavens simply "the accuser" in a courtroom context? The text is certainly indicating a role that the being then performs, but the English translations that provide the proper noun "Satan" are not mistaken. Canon clarifies. Revelation 12:10 includes this phrase in reference to Satan (v. 9), "for the accuser of our brothers and sisters has been thrown down, the one who accuses them before our God day and night." Who is "the accuser" in the heavens? The author of Revelation relays a voice from heaven who declares the accuser to be Satan, and that piece of canonical commentary clarifies the heavenly accusation texts of Job 1–2 and Zechariah

---

12. Hartley, *Book of Job*, 71.

3. Commenting on Revelation 12:10, Robert Mounce sees the connection with Job: "Satan's role as the greater accuser, as we have seen, finds classic expression in the book of Job (1:6–12; 2:1–5; cf. 1 Enoch 40:7). His accusations against the righteous continue night and day. But by virtue of the death of Christ he is unable successfully to lodge a charge against God's elect (Rom 8:33–34)."[13] While providing the name Satan in the books of Job and Zechariah is not necessarily a perfect translation choice, it appears to be theologically sound.

Returning to Job, in each exchange, Satan's mobility throughout heaven and earth is evident. He wanders the earth, presumably watching events and persons. He is also present before God in this great council. Ironically, many perceive him as the resident and ruler of hell or the underworld, but neither Job nor any other text portrays such a home for him before the final judgments. Satan's wandering status gives him a general understanding of Job and his blessed situation.

Satan in his first speech berates God for buying Job's allegiance with blessings. Hartley comments, "But the Satan questioned God's praise of Job. He doubted whether any person would fear God for nothing or without reason. . . . The Satan's question insinuated that all good deeds spring from selfish motives. To him this would surely be true in Job's case, for Yahweh had both protected Job from all harm and blessed him abundantly."[14] By questioning Job's motives, Satan is knocking on the door of heaven, so to speak, that he might gain access to Job's estate and afflict him. As the narrative recounts, Satan succeeds in his effort to harm Job after questioning the man's motives before God. Yet the Lord ensures that his own intentions toward Job will prevail in the end.

Satan entreats God a second time because Job did not waver at the loss of his possessions and children, and Satan uses the same line of disbelief. Hartley continues, "The Satan persisted in his skeptical attitude about the grounds of Job's faith. He posited that Job was acting contritely because he had not really been tested."[15] Satan is determined to prove that the faith of God's protected people is only a sham; they are only blessing God because of reciprocity.

Do we perceive the audacity of Satan? Like a tenacious prosecutor before an immovable judge, Satan suggests God's complicity even as he commands the Lord of all creation to act. "Reach out your hand," he demands. While the holy sons of God diligently present themselves and submit to the will of God,

---

13. Robert H. Mounce, *The Book of Revelation*, New International Commentary on the New Testament (Grand Rapids: Eerdmans, 1997), 238.

14. Hartley, *Book of Job*, 73.

15. Hartley, 80.

Satan brazenly acts according to his own will and purpose – the humiliation of God through the shaming of his people.

The Whisper to Eliphaz in the Night

> Can mankind be righteous before God?
> Can a man be pure before his Maker?
> He puts no trust even in His servants;
> And He accuses His angels of error.
> How much more those who live in houses of clay,
> Whose foundation is in the dust,
> Who are crushed before the moth!
> Between morning and evening they are broken in pieces;
> Unregarded, they perish forever.
> Is their tent-cord not pulled up within them?
> They die, yet without wisdom. (Job 4:17–21)

Eliphaz is the first of Job's friends to respond after Job's poetic laments of chapter three. His intentions are immediately evident: he intends to undermine Job's character to explain these horrific circumstances. In Job 4:7, he says, "Remember now, who *ever* perished being innocent? Or where were the upright destroyed?" But the attack continues.

During his speech against Job, Eliphaz recounts the words told to him in a dream (Job 4:12–16), words "brought to [him] secretly" by a "spirit." Drawing from what that spirit said (Job 4:17–21), this "friend" insists that Job's guilt is the cause of Job's downfall. Hartley summarizes the spirit's conclusions with these lines, "No human or heavenly creature is just, i.e. righteous, in relationship to God."[16] Yet was Eliphaz's dreadful encounter an interaction with a demonic presence? The text does not give many details, and the meeting was less of a vision to see than a disturbance to hear. But Eliphaz "did get a glimpse of something resembling a spirit."[17] While the Hebrew word translated "spirit" could represent a mere wind, the context and poetical structure lead us to believe that a "form" of a being was present.[18]

Was it a demon, or some other kind of spirit or angel? The demonic qualities of this spirit are evident. First, it supplies Eliphaz with supernatural

---

16. Hartley, 111.
17. Hartley, 111.
18. Alden, *Job*, 87.

material to accuse Job and strengthen his argument, operating in concert with Satan's work. Second, while the Lord spoke in a quiet whisper to Elijah in 1 Kings 19:12–13, the narrative flow of the book of Job does not suggest that a parallel event occurs here. The origin of this whisper is not divine. Third, Old Testament appearances of holy angels are not whispery or vague (see Gen 19:1; 2 Kgs 6:16–17; Dan 6:22). So this was not one of them. Fourth, the content of this spirit's testimony is curious, containing some uncommon information about angels being judged. Therefore, a demon, a rebellious angel, is the most plausible option.

This demonic speech serves as the seed for Eliphaz's opinion concerning his friend Job. After the introductory questions to broach the topic, the spirit uses a self-referential example to support the condemnation of human beings. If God holds the angels accountable (2 Pet 2:4), surely the eye of the pure, unrelenting God scrutinizes and condemns human beings!

Satan challenges God in the heavenlies concerning Job and secures the right to afflict him. A demon whispers condemnation about Job on the earth, with no concept of redemption or hope attached.[19] The whole picture is this: Satan and his minion mix accusation, deception, and affliction to produce a poisonous cocktail, tempting Job to reject God.

The Deceiver of Ahab

> And the LORD said, "Who will entice Ahab to go up and fall at Ramoth-gilead?" And one *spirit* said this, while another said that. Then a spirit came forward and stood before the LORD, and said, "**I will entice him** [Ahab]." And the LORD said to him, "How?" And he said, "**I will go out and be a deceiving spirit in the mouths of all his prophets.**" Then He said, "You shall entice him, and you will also prevail. Go and do so." (1 Kgs 22:20–22)[20]

All the signs proved favorable for war. But the good King Jehoshaphat of Judah insisted that he and King Ahab of Israel needed further guidance. Even though all the prophets predicted their victory in battle at Ramoth-gilead, Jehoshaphat requested the counsel of a prophet of the Lord. The shrewd prophet Micaiah reveals the reason for the unanimous predictions of the other prophets by

---

19. As there is no biblical instance of the redemption of a demon, one could expect the omission of the subject by ignorance as well as by intention.

20. Also 2 Chronicles 18:20–21. The difference between the recording of the spirit's speech in the two passages is negligible.

telling of his vision of the divine throne room in the heavenlies. God and his host were not "plotting strategies to go to war on behalf of Israel, but instead the discussion is directed against Ahab," the notoriously wicked king over the northern tribes.[21]

Before his heavenly court of supernatural beings, the Lord had justly ruled that Ahab must die and sentenced him to death in battle. But who would entice Ahab to go into this disastrous battle where he would meet his death? A spirit volunteers to be a deceiving spirit in the prophets' mouths.[22] It is difficult to ascertain if these other prophets were demonized, but the certainty is this: "The lying prophets were not just deceitful men but men inspired by demons."[23] The demon deceives, yet ultimately the Lord fulfills his righteous purpose of removing Ahab.

The Tempter of Christ

> And the tempter came and said to Him, "**If You are the Son of God, command that these stones become bread.**" (Matt 4:3)
>
> And he said to Him, "**If You are the Son of God, throw Yourself down; for it is written, 'He will give His angels orders concerning You'; and 'On their hands they will lift You up, So that You do not strike Your foot against a stone.'**" (Matt 4:6, 9)
>
> And he said to Him, "**All these things** [kingdoms of the world] **I will give You, if You fall down and worship me.**" (Matt 4:9)
>
> And the devil said to Him, "**I will give You all this domain and its glory, for it has been handed over to me, and I give it to whomever I want. Therefore if You worship before me, it shall all be Yours.**" (Luke 4:6–7)[24]

No accusation arises here. What could Satan point out? Like he did in the garden, except that the location is more difficult (a wilderness devoid of sustenance), Satan is attacking an innocent target, a person free of sin. He

---

21. Walton, Matthews, and Chavalas, *IVP Bible Background Commentary*, 439.

22. While some cases arouse debate (e.g. Judg 9:23), the idea of somehow rejecting this spirit as a demonic being is contextually difficult and unpalatable.

23. Thompson, *1, 2 Chronicles*, 286.

24. The order of the temptations is different in Luke, and the temptation of rulership over the nations has more content.

wields unmitigated deception and temptation as he lunges at the Son of God three times.

Satan appeals to the human desire of Jesus to avoid suffering. This desert is no Eden, where fruit was plentiful and only one tree was forbidden. Jesus's stomach is empty. He could not quickly reject Satan's advances by reaching for another food source. His human frame is frail and spent after forty days of fasting. Hagner describes the situation well:

> To turn the stones into bread would be in effect to refuse God's will and would involve a disobedience that would belie Jesus' sonship. . . . The testing then amounts to this: shall Jesus exercise his messianic power for his own ends in a way that voids difficulty and pain, or shall he accept the path of suffering (and death) that is his Father's will?[25]

The second temptation follows a similar tack. Satan knows that the Son can summon all the angels of heaven. Satan urges Jesus to jump ahead and use that power, which would have meant that Jesus chose to reject the Father's ordained path of "danger and suffering."[26]

The third (or second in Luke) temptation is an effort to tempt and turn Christ from his mission. In the past, Satan had received dominion over the nations (Luke 4:6). Now before Jesus, he presents a shortcut to the "messianic glory," a cutting of corners by which Jesus could be great on earth without suffering and death.[27] And clearly Satan is interested in receiving worship in place of the rightful recipient of adoration – his Creator! Yet the words of Satan, of crafty deception and timely temptation, prove ineffective.

The Defensive Spirit of Capernaum

> In the synagogue there was a man possessed by the spirit of an unclean demon, and he cried out with a loud voice, **"Let us alone! What business do You have with us, Jesus of Nazareth? Have You come to destroy us? I know who You are – the Holy One of God!"** (Luke 4:33–34)[28]

---

25. Hagner, *Matthew 1–13*, 65.
26. Hagner, 67.
27. John Nolland, *Luke 1–9:20* (Nashville: Thomas Nelson, 1989), 180.
28. Also Mark 1:24. Mark's version is the same, except it omits, "Let us alone!"

In his gospel, Mark adopts an unusual course in his introduction of Jesus. In 1:7–8, John the Baptist testifies that Jesus is the Christ. In 1:11, the Father declares from the heavens that Jesus is his "beloved Son." But then in 1:24, an unclean spirit speaks and testifies of Jesus's identity! This surprising contribution from the demonic realm breaks from the exorcism stories of the time. A typical exorcist would solicit a name from the demon to gain authority over the spirit.[29] Instead, the demon states, "What business do you have with us?" or "What do we have in common?" Guelich asserts, "The question betrays the unclean spirit's recognition of his own status, particularly in the light of Jesus' authority."[30]

Instead of Jesus using the spirit's name to expel it, the demon gives a name of Jesus – "The Holy One of God." But the demon is not overtly trying to gain the upper hand, though the commotion it caused could have escalated and disturbed Jesus's developing messianic ministry. The demon's statement is an admission of its complete inferiority. "The demon recognized the deity and, as in Mark 1:24 and 5:7, acknowledges the exorcist to be superior. Therefore, this announcement shows the demon's awareness of who Jesus is and that Jesus is his superior. . . . In so doing he identifies Jesus for Mark's audience or reader."[31] Thus, it is no surprise that the situation resolves with but a few words, convulsions, and a cry – without the extravagant rituals and tools frequently found in ancient accounts of exorcisms.

The supernatural, heavenly knowledge of this spirit warrants reflection. The efforts to demythologize or depersonalize demonic beings do not fit with the words of this unclean spirit. It squirms as a lesser power before a greater Power, persons who are acquainted with one another. Who could suppose this reaction to be of a human spirit or an impersonal force? When accepted, the text makes all such hypotheses out of bounds.

Finally, the demon was expecting something from Jesus. Its speech exposes the broken relationship between them. The spirit expects judgment. It knows its role, as well as who will exert his dominion over the fallen powers in the end.

---

29. In general, biblical exorcisms do not require the discovery of a demon's name. Apart from Jesus with the Gerasene demoniac, no other exorcist in the Scripture requests a name. Exorcists need not belabor the search for names when they can also address a spirit by behavior/symptoms: "You mute and deaf spirit" (Mark 9:25).

30. Guelich, *Mark 1–8:26*, 57.

31. Guelich, 57.

The Unclean Spirits' Testimony

> Demons also were coming out of many, shouting, "**You are the Son of God!**" (Luke 4:41a)[32]

The shouts of these demons seem good, do they not? Jesus is healing people, among whom are demonized persons. Yet as Jesus casts out these spirits, the demons shout, "You are the Son of God!" They are attempting to pull back the veil of the Christ's ministry.

Their testimony is correct, but it is counterproductive. So Jesus silences them, just as he shushed some people after he healed them (Mark 1:44). Consider the consequences: how would the Son of God, the Messiah be known? Would he be known as a miracle worker, an exorcist, or something else? Nolland states, "Jesus is only rightly known as Christ in connection with His sufferings."[33] At this early stage of his ministry, Jesus has yet to reveal his full work, so he protects his identity! Christ himself regulates the dispensing of those details.

The Legion before Christ

> And when He came to the other side into the country of the Gadarenes, two demon-possessed men confronted Him as they were coming out of the tombs. They were so extremely violent that no one could pass by that way. And they cried out, saying, "**What business do You have with us, Son of God? Have You come here to torment us before the time?**" . . . And the demons begged Him, saying, "**If You are going to cast us out, send us into the herd of pigs.**" (Matt 8:28–29, 31)

> Seeing Jesus from a distance, he [the demoniac] ran up and bowed down before Him; and shouting with a loud voice, he said, "**What business do you have with me, Jesus, Son of the Most High God? I implore You by God, do not torment me!**" . . . And He was asking him, "What is your name?" And he said to Him, "**My name is Legion; for we are many.**" . . . And the demons begged Him, saying, "**Send us into the pigs so that we may enter them.**" (Mark 5:6–7, 9, 12)

---

32. Also Mark 3:11. The records of Mark and Luke are identical.
33. Nolland, *Luke 1–9:20*, 214.

> And seeing Jesus, he cried out and fell down before Him, and said with a loud voice, "**What business do you have with me, Jesus, Son of the Most High God? I beg You, do not torment me!**" . . . And Jesus asked him, "What is your name?" And he said, "**Legion**"; because many demons had entered him. (Luke 8:28, 30)

Similar to the synagogue spirit, this legion of demons verbally submits to the "Son of the Most High God," a telling title employed in the Mark and Luke versions. This name "underlines the gentile setting of the story."[34] Even in a world under the dominion of demonic "gods," all spirits yield to the Supreme.

Again, the demons acknowledge their place, expecting judgment. No doubt, they had long considered the prophesies of old such as Isaiah 24 that foretell their doom. The legion of demons even knows that torture awaits them, which Revelation 20:10 describes in relation to Satan. Yet something seems out of kilter to them. Hagner summarizes, "First, in it the demons recognize that at the eschatological judgment they will experience God's judgment and the end of their power . . . and second, they recognize that . . . [the] 'time,' has not yet come; Jesus has in effect come too early and threatens their realm too soon."[35] Though Mark and Luke leave out the detail about the "time," that pinch of surprise seasons the whole conversation.

The final pleadings of the demons involve a nearby herd of pigs. If one assumes that the best condition for a demon is inhabiting a being, and that going to the abyss would be the worst condition, the pigs are an option for the spirits to remain together, at least until the pigs suddenly commit suicide![36] The sudden death of the animals could also mean that the demons intended to become free spirits. Confronted by Jesus, they feared torture and the abyss, and perhaps they believed that Jesus would not expel them into freedom or another human. The pigs served as a nearby refuge where they could avoid the abyss and reside momentarily before moving on to better prospects.

The conclusion of the story appears to be incomplete. Yes, Jesus sets the man free by defeating the demons. However, the demons escape, for their final destruction is yet to come.

---

34. Guelich, *Mark 1–8:26*, 279.

35. Hagner, *Matthew 1–13*, 227.

36. Aside from inhabitation being the best condition of an evil spirit, inhabitation can also be the best strategy. Satan's inhabitation of Judas, one of the Twelve, was surely for strategic purposes in arranging the betrayal and arrest of the Christ.

The Spirit Seeking a Home

> [Jesus said] "When the unclean spirit comes out of a person, it passes through waterless places seeking rest, and not finding any, it then says, '**I will return to my house from which I came.**' And when it comes, it finds it swept and put in order. Then it goes and brings along seven other spirits more evil than itself, and they come in and live there; and the last condition of that person becomes worse than the first." (Luke 11:24–26)[37]

Jesus knows the behavior of demons and their thoughts. He tells a story, likely fictitious yet grounded in real experiences like the rest of his storying ministry, about a demon who has left a man. In contrast with how concrete transformation happens in the kingdom of God (11:20–23), here a demonized person encounters a seemingly fortunate turn in life, but it is merely temporary freedom before the spirit returns with worse companions. Change outside the kingdom of God often leads to greater bondage.

In this narrative, Jesus shares the perspective of the wandering demon. The spirit is on "a journey of exploration to hunt out a better lair," desiring a better residence.[38] But it finds nothing. What does it do? Initially, having evaluated its situation and options, it makes a choice, "I will return," and claims a location, "to my house from which I came," like a tenant in a dilapidated rental who has no other options. From Jesus's lips, this account is a brief yet insightful glimpse into the wicked activities of inhabiting spirits.

The Syncretizing Spirit of Philippi

> It happened that as we were going to the place of prayer, a slave woman who had a spirit of divination met us, who was bringing great profit to her masters by fortune-telling. She followed Paul and us and cried out repeatedly, saying, "**These men are bondservants of the Most High God, who are proclaiming to you a way of salvation.**" (Acts 16:16–17)

Returning to exorcisms in the gentile context, a demon, literally a "python spirit," is accosting Paul. What is this spirit? Keener explains, "This slave girl (as in 12:13, the Greek implies that she is very young) has literally a 'spirit

---

37. Also Matt 12:43–45, which is nearly identical to Luke's account.
38. John Nolland, *Luke 9:21–18:34* (Dallas: Word, 1993), 647.

of a pythoness' – the same sort of spirit that stood behind the most famous of all Greek oracles, the Delphic oracle of Apollo."[39] Meanwhile, the apostle is focusing on his mission of delivering the gospel, and for "many days," he ignores the spirit. But the demonized girl continues to repeat the same words, over and over, producing their desired effect.

What is the spirit's aim? Several options are possible. First, the spirit is primarily interested in annoying the missionaries and slowing their ministry. F. F. Bruce represents this perspective: "The missionaries, however, did not appreciate her unsolicited testimonials, and at last Paul, vexed by her continual clamor, exorcized the spirit that possessed her."[40] But this view does not explain why the demon would share this particular information!

Second, the spirit is primarily interested in promoting pluralism, creating confusion as to who the "Most High God" is and how many ways to God or of salvation exist. For example, the "Most High God" could refer to Zeus in a Greek language context.[41] And as the NASB translates and Polhill suggests, the text could read "*a* way of salvation," which suggests there are multiple ways to God.[42] Perhaps the demon is trying to present the gospel Paul was preaching as just another option.

Third, the spirit is primarily interested in creating syncretism, or the mixing of religious ideas. The presence of the demonized girl who is textually associated with the oracle of Delphi as having a python spirit could lead people to accept both the testimonies of the demon and of the apostle. In other words, what if people heed the word of the python spirit and then follow Paul? The people accepting two spiritual authorities would fall into syncretism.

The second and third options are the most plausible when we view the demonic speech against the missional backdrop. In either of these options, syncretism caused by demonic deception is a danger, for by operating as an announcer of the apostle's identity and message, the spirit ensures that their association with the Greek god of the Delphi oracle is inevitable. Paul's reaction and exorcism are right and necessary since the exorcism demonstrates the superiority and exclusivity of the gospel. Christianity cannot be connected to gentile polytheism.

---

39. Keener, *IVP Bible Background Commentary: New Testament*, 370.

40. F. F. Bruce, *The Book of the Acts*, New International Commentary on the New Testament (Grand Rapids: Eerdmans, 1988), 313.

41. Polhill, *Acts*, 351.

42. Polhill, 351.

The Unmastered Spirit of Ephesus

> But also some of the Jewish exorcists, who went from place to place, attempted to use the name of the Lord Jesus over those who had the evil spirits, saying, "I order you in the name of Jesus whom Paul preaches!" Now there were seven sons of Sceva, a Jewish chief priest, doing this. But the evil spirit responded and said to them, "**I recognize Jesus, and I know of Paul, but who are you?**" And the man in whom was the evil spirit, pounced on them and subdued all of them and overpowered them, so that they fled out of that house naked and wounded. (Acts 19:13–16)

Ephesus was a spiritual minefield. The worship of Artemis gripped the city. The use of magic was pervasive. Exorcism was big business! Sceva's sons, with their deliverance ministry, were likely eager to make a name for themselves which can be seen in their claiming the dubious title of sons of the "Jewish high priest," which was probably a "self-designation, set out on a placard: Luke might have placed the words between quotation marks had those been invented in his day."[43] But in a context where names mean power, this title conveyed much.

> The Jewish high priest was the one man who was authorized to pronounce the otherwise ineffable name [the Tetragrammaton name of God]; this he did once a year, in the course of the service prescribed for the day of atonement. Such a person would therefore enjoy high prestige among magicians. It was not the ineffable name, however, but the name of Jesus that Sceva's sons employed in their attempt to imitate Paul's exorcizing ministry.[44]

What a tangle for the early missionaries to unweave! By the miraculous work of God, Paul's apostolic ministry was given authority by "extraordinary" signs, which paved the way for the gospel to be accepted in the religiously and demonically entrenched city (Acts 19:11–12). Yet the city was trembling before a spiritual explosion.

The magicians publicly exposed their spell books and magical paraphernalia, rendering them useless, and further destroyed them by fire (Acts 19:17–20). What caused them to abandon the practices of their ancestors and community? Sceva's sons waded into waters out of their depth. Presumably to replicate the spiritual strength of Paul's ministry, they self-servingly used the name of

---

43. Bruce, *Book of the Acts*, 368.
44. Bruce, 369.

Jesus, with whom they had no relationship. The result was predictable: "Like an unfamiliar weapon wrongly handled it exploded in their hands."[45]

The demonic speech exposed their error. The demon knew Jesus, as the demons of the Gospels testify. The beings in the spiritual realm had heard about Paul, though he was perhaps not as widely known as the Son of God. When encountering this spirit, the sons of Sceva learned that the name of Jesus is not a magic charm one dangles before a demon, because the spirit attacked the worthless men. The event prompted many to fear the name of Jesus and caused further upheaval in Ephesus, dramatic demonstrations of repentance from magic practices and turning to faith in Jesus.

Lessons for the Church

According to our goal of presenting a demonology for the global church, what lessons can we gather from these twelve passages of demonic speech? While we could offer more, here are four lessons for the benefit of God's people. Let us study to persevere.

1. Submission. The relationship between God and the demonic host is set. They are inferior and submissive to the Creator of the visible and invisible.
2. Ontology. From their own words, the demons operate as real, supernatural beings who are aware of heavenly and earthly beings.
3. Personhood. While the activities of demons include orchestrating and empowering various systems of evil, demons are not these systems. They interact as persons within systems and promote strategies.
4. Activities. The speeches of demons in the Bible provides exceptional examples of their core activities.

In the global context, challenges to the nature and personhood of demons are common. Dualistic, Manichaean ideas that portray good and evil powers as locked in a perpetual struggle for supremacy persist. These anti-biblical philosophies exalt the power of the demonic and diminish divine sovereignty. Exaggerating and minimizing the activities of demons is commonplace as well. This look at the speech of demons is a needed corrective that supports our

---

45. Bruce, 369.

previous analysis of the activity of demons and our upcoming study of their nature and personhood.

The Quiet Exit

The biblical canon's record of demonic speech ends with the events in Ephesus in Acts. Of course, they and their handiwork continue to be discussed throughout the remainder of the biblical witness. As we think about these foul agents of unrighteousness and their discourse, we confront this reality: We hear their voices every day in the dogma, accusations, and deceptions of our age. The foolish arrogance of these beings, their bold tricks, and their whispers of accusation are still part of earthly life. But Revelation 20:10 shouts their future: "And the devil who deceived them was thrown into the lake of fire and brimstone, where the beast and the false prophet are also; and they will be tormented day and night forever and ever."[46] From clashes in the heavenlies to anguish in the lake of fire, what else can Satan and the demonic host say? They are gone without a word.

---

46. Mounce states, "In the preceding chapter the beast and false prophet were cast into the fiery lake of burning sulfur (19:20). They are now joined . . . by the arch culprit, the devil himself." Mounce, *The Book of Revelation*, 374.

6

The Nature of Demons

After our survey of the various activities and speeches of demons, the reasonable response may be who or what are these demons? In addressing the nature or ontological qualities of demons, we will delve into their attributes before discussing issues relating to personhood. What is their nature? What are their abilities? Are demons personal beings? These and other questions loom, and only after a survey of their behavior and speech in the Bible should we address these significant topics.

Are Demons "Real?"

At first glance, the question "Are demons real?" may appear absurd for a couple of reasons. Some of us scoff at the question because our worldview assumptions have forced a hasty dismissal of the reality of demons altogether. Yet others of us scoff because the question is a given. "Of course demons are real!" we say. "How could someone possibly deny it?" Especially after our walk through the Scriptures looking at the activity and speech of demons, it is rather contrary to suggest that the Bible is not arguing for, or at least supporting the existence of demons, beings who interact with God, angels, and human beings.

Yet some propose that demons are not "real." They argue that perhaps the word of God speaks figuratively about demons and other spiritual beings, that they are personifications of evil forces, or that the accounts of them are myths. Could demons be literary features of a bygone era, part of myths which have little bearing on existence?

Let us reflect on Friedrich Schleiermacher's conception of demons as a literary archetype. Seeing the angelic realm as a myth, he insists, "Previously there was no alternative but to people either the earth or the heavens with hidden and spiritual beings."[1] Schleiermacher's alternative view is startling. Concerning the angels, he says:

> Christ and the Apostles might have said all these things without having had any real conviction of the existence of such beings or any desire to communicate it, just as everyone adopts popular ideas and makes use of them in discussing other things, as, for example, we might talk of ghosts and fairies, although these ideas had no definite sort of relation to our actual convictions.[2]

Though the idea of angels continues in hymns, confessions, and Scripture, he leaves the reality of the angelic host as an unanswered and unimportant question, supposing that Christians will be less influenced by the subject as human "knowledge of the forces of nature" increases.[3]

It should then prove unsurprising that Schleiermacher's skepticism overflows into demons and Satan. "The idea of the Devil, as developed among us, is so unstable that we cannot expect anyone to be convinced of its truth."[4] He again argues that such concepts will become "obsolete" in Christian usage as we continue to better understand "evil emotions" that arise within us in a "strange and abrupt manner."[5] Schleiermacher culminates his view of demons by arguing that as long as such references to evil are the norm in Christian circles, they can also be reflected in song. This lyrical usage is apparently appropriate since "in poetry personification is quite in place."[6] Rather than a complete removal of the subject from church life, Schleiermacher says it is "unjustifiable to wish to banish the conception of the devil from our treasury of song."[7]

Unfortunately, many others agree with Schleiermacher, in part or whole, and consider demons to be something less than created spiritual beings with power, ability, and intelligence. For example, Karl Barth's perspective on the "origin and nature" of demons as "nothingness" is troublesome.[8] Barth burdens his analysis of biblical texts with a philosophical concept that is foreign to the Scriptures. Thankfully, Barth does not toss aside demons as unreal; according

---

1. Friedrich Schleiermacher, *The Christian Faith* (Edinburgh: T & T Clark, 1928), 157.
2. Schleiermacher, *Christian Faith*, 158.
3. Schleiermacher, 159.
4. Schleiermacher, 161.
5. Schleiermacher, 168.
6. Schleiermacher, 169–70.
7. Schleiermacher, 170.
8. Barth, *Church Dogmatics*, III, 3, 522.

to Barth, no one can hurt demons by "questioning their existence."[9] But though he asserts that demons are real, Barth insists that they are not part of God's original, pristine creation. Rather he treats them as a complex byproduct of the creation decree.[10] By creating, the act inevitably spawned the negation – the "nothingness" – that is the demonic. Yet, by speaking about demons in biblical ways concerning their activities and speech, Barth simultaneously constructs demons as personal beings yet undermines their existence as creatures.

However, this creative interpretation does not fit with biblical truth. As Bromiley reasons, Barth "lays himself open to criticism at a vital point: Is he really obeying scripture as the criterion of dogmatic purity and truth?"[11] Instead, as we study the Scriptures, they do identify the nature of demons, and they present the demonic host as fallen creatures. Demons are not the reactionary spawn of the creation decree, nor are they mere personifications of powerful forces, a wordplay to explain the existence of impersonal evils. Aiming to portray reality, the Scriptures call them spirits, as it does the angels.[12] The meticulous Luke, in the genre of historical narrative, provides this clarity as he uses "demon" and "spirit" synonymously in the same passages.

> In the synagogue there was a man possessed by the *spirit* of an unclean *demon*, and he cried out with a loud voice. (Luke 4:33)[13]
>
> He had already commanded the unclean *spirit* to come out of the man. For it had seized him many times; and he was bound with chains and shackles and kept under guard, and yet he would break his bonds and be driven by the *demon* into the desert. (Luke 8:29)
>
> While he was still approaching, the *demon* slammed him to the ground and threw him into a convulsion. But Jesus rebuked the unclean *spirit*, and healed the boy and gave him back to his father. (Luke 9:42)[14]

---

9. Barth, 521.

10. Barth, 523.

11. Bromiley, *Introduction to the Theology of Karl Barth*, 155.

12. See Heb 1:14: "Are [holy angels] not all ministering spirits, sent out to provide service for the sake of those who will inherit salvation?"

13. Nolland states, "Having in mind the use in Acts 17:18 of [*daimonion*] for 'deity,' it is perhaps best to see Luke as establishing here his basic vocabulary for possession . . . and in the negative sphere [spirit and demon] are interchangeable." Nolland, *Luke 1–9:20*, 206.

14. According to Nolland, "Corresponding to the highly personal and heart-rending appeal of the father for his only child, Luke here speaks simply, but powerfully, of Jesus healing the child and handing him over to his father. The note of compassion comes strongly to the fore. Luke

Furthermore, the content of their speech sets the demons apart. Given their knowledge of Jesus as the Son of God and their fear of judgment, demons as they are depicted in the Bible do not qualify as mere moods or psychological aberrations. They are spirits who are alien to the human realm of existence.

Yet "spirits," a term which encompasses both angels (Heb 1:14) and demons, are not spirits in the sense that God is the Spirit. In Kato's booklet on the spirits, he states, "God as Spirit is absolutely different from all other classes of spirits. He is the Creator.... So in our dealing with the origin of spirits, we must exclude God. Although he too is Spirit, he is the uncreated Spirit since he himself did the creating. All other spirits are created beings."[15] Demons are finite, evil spirits who exist under the sovereignty and supremacy of the Infinite Spirit. While we should avoid associating angels and demons because of the opposite moral characteristics that distinguish each group, they do share the nature of existing as finite spirits created by God. In some sense, the similarity of the two groups reflects a distinction that is like the pre-fall Adam and post-fall Adam. Both natures of Adam are human, consisting of flesh and spirit. But the differences between pre-fall and post-fall Adam are numerous and monumental. So although they are very different from holy angels, demons are spirits, and attempts to describe them as impersonal powers or psychological manifestations do harm to the integrity of the biblical text.

What Is the Origin of Demons?

While we can discern a little about the origin of demons, Scripture seems unconcerned to discuss the matter at length. But the cultures of the world have always manufactured explanations. Perhaps demons are restless human ancestors or disembodied human-angel chimeras? The Bible does not support either idea. Again, we must remain true to the biblical testimony and its emphases.

The angelic host (the sons of God) are ancient. In Job 38:1–7, the Lord chastises Job by reminding the man that he was not present when God laid the foundations of the world. Job could not claim knowledge of the event; he was not a witness. But verse 7 states that the "sons of God," the angels, sang and shouted during the creation of the earth. Hartley explains the significance of this text.

---

is happy to use the language of healing for exorcisms, but this does not mean that he confuses illness and exorcism." Nolland, *Luke 9:21–18:34*, 510.

15. Kato, *What the Bible Teaches*, 4.

> In an ancient community the laying of a foundation stone for a public building such as a temple was a high occasion and was commemorated by a festive ceremony. On the occasion of laying the earth's cornerstone, *the morning stars* were assembled as an angelic chorus to sing praises to God for the glory of his world. At the moment the stone was set in place *the sons of God*, i.e., the angels, broke out in joyous singing, praising God, the Creator. Since no human being was present at this occasion, the inner structure of the universe remains a secret hidden from mankind.[16]

As for how long the angelic host existed prior to that event, the Scriptures do not say. But the realm of the invisible powers is older than humanity.

What about demons? The entrance of sin among the heavenly powers took place prior to humanity's fall, as evidenced by the deception of the serpent. We should not assume that one spiritual being would act alone. Throughout Christian history, the church has looked to Revelation 12:1–4 for guidance concerning this rebellion. Some object, claiming that "the language of Rev 12:1–9 is clearly set at the first advent (Rev 12:4–5)."[17] But the timing of events in Revelation is no certain matter. Furthermore, the fact that Satan and his angels vacated heaven at some point does not mean that they were without fault prior to this event. Satan surely was not! Rather in Revelation 12, the holy angels displace the presumably ancient coalition, whatever the timing of the expulsion may be.

Some of the corrupt angels are responsible for the evils described in Genesis 6 and are presently imprisoned. And as we read the narratives in 1 Kings 22 and Job 1–2, we begin to see how God uses these evil powers for his purposes on earth. With various roles, abilities, and locations, these demons are the rebellious angels – no extra-canonical, cultural explanations necessary.

Do Demons Have a Body?

This question is also difficult to answer from the Scriptures. We cannot find a definite conclusion, but we can glean some direction. First, Satan and his demons possess the ability to manifest in various forms. But this flexibility clouds the exact nature of their being. In Paul's explanation of how false teachers masquerade as true apostles, he writes, "For such men are false

---

16. Hartley, *The Book of Job*, 495. Emphasis original.
17. Heiser, *Demons*, 110.

apostles, deceitful workers, disguising themselves as apostles of Christ. No wonder, for even Satan disguises himself as an angel of light. Therefore it is not surprising if his servants also disguise themselves as servants of righteousness, whose end will be according to their deeds" (2 Cor 11:13–15).[18] If we combine this comparison with the indwelling capabilities of demons, we should carefully weigh and test our interactions with spirits and people, even if they are visually respectable. Lacking discernment, we could easily imitate the naivety of our ancestors in the garden.

Second, demons likely have the ability to manifest physically or "actualize" into the seen realm. Apart from indwelling a physical being, spirits can appear and interact in the earthly realm. For example when holy angels visited Abraham and Lot in Genesis 18–19, they ate and conversed as humans.[19] Similarly when the devil arrived to tempt Christ in the wilderness, one possible conclusion is that he presented himself in a physical form to interact with Jesus. However, even though demons can appear in various forms and they can be localized entities (as we saw in our study of Daniel 10), we simply do not have enough biblical material to conclude whether or not they have a physical body of some kind.

Are Demons All the Same?

No, demons are not all the same. Satan and his demons are all engaged in evil activities, yet some distinctions exist between them. One example is in their varying levels of evil. In addition to 1 Peter 3:19, 2 Peter 2:4 and Jude 1:6 mention the exceptionally abhorrent spirits who are imprisoned spirits.[20] Jesus gives some unusually specific information about demonic traits in Luke.

---

18. Garland states, "Satan can pose as an angel of light. It should not be surprising then if satanic evil infiltrates a church and deludes it. The argument runs, if Satan disguises himself with the raiment of righteousness, then so will his minions. The rivals are no different from the master they serve." Garland, *2 Corinthians*, 485.

19. Genesis 18:8 depicts them eating, but it is not until 19:1 that the two beside the Lord are identified as angels. Lest we merely reckon them to be human messengers, we observe their unusual abilities in 19:11 when they repel the lustful men of the city. Mathews states, "Unlike the suddenness of the visitors' appearance before Abraham, hinting at their otherworldly origin . . . the angels are received simply as common travelers without any detection by Lot. Not until the angels blind the Sodomites do they show their supernatural character (vv. 10–11)." Mathews, *Genesis 1–11:26*, 233.

20. According to Achtemeier, "In the NT the word 'spirits' . . . is used overwhelmingly to refer not to human dead but to supernatural beings, primarily malevolent. . . . There is a clear Jewish tradition . . . in which the angelic beings of Gen 6:1–6, whose disobedience caused the flood, were subsequently imprisoned. . . . That it is this tradition which underlies the reference

> When the unclean spirit goes out of a person, it passes through waterless places seeking rest, and not finding any, it then says, "I will return to my house from which I came." And when it comes, it finds it swept and put in order. Then it goes and takes along seven other spirits more evil than itself, and they come in and live there; and the last condition of that person becomes worse than the first. (Luke 11:24–26)

In this parable of Jesus, a demon that has exited a host tries to find a place to rest. In the end, it chooses to return to its now cleaned prior abode, and a demonic mob joins it. But the new associates are more evil than the first demon, and the dramatic increase of demonic residents and the intensity of their evil further damages the man. Nolland adds, "The returning demon provides himself with a whole set of demonic companions, each of whom outstrips the original dweller's capacity to inflict evil upon its host."[21] So some demons are worse than others. In this sense, demons mirror humanity. All are sinners, but some are more scandalously prolific in quantity, intensity, and craftiness.

We can also distinguish demons by their various states and locations. The information in the teaching of Jesus in Luke 11:24–26 illustrates that a demon can indwell a person, but it can also be a transient spirit with no host. And as mentioned earlier, demons can take on a physical shape and interact in a physical manner. But only "free" or operational spirits have all of these attributes. These evil spirits are distinct from the bound, inoperative spirits who are not able to return to earth, according to Jude 1:6.

Evil spirits also have different ranks and roles, and the Bible portrays Satan as the leader of the demonic horde. First, Revelation 12 describes "the dragon and his angels" warring in a grand battle with the archangel Michael and his angels, indicating Satan's exalted position over the fallen angels and their loyalty to him (Rev 12:7).[22] Second, though we will avoid speculation,

---

to 'spirits' in our verse seems therefore likely to be the case." Paul J. Achtemeier, *1 Peter: A Commentary on First Peter*, Hermeneia (Minneapolis: Fortress, 1995), 255–56. Schreiner asserts, "We can be almost certain that Jude referred here to the sin of the angels in Gen 6:1–4." Schreiner, *1, 2 Peter, Jude*, 448. In a survey of the positions taken on the text in 1 Peter 3:19, Bauckham states, "Second, the 'spirits in prison' are angelic beings, which the word 'spirits' alone (rather than 'spirits of . . .') probably most naturally suggests (though human spirits is not at all an impossible meaning of the word)." Richard Bauckham, "Spirits in Prison," in *The Anchor Bible Dictionary*, ed. D. N. Freedman, vol. 6 (New York: Doubleday, 1992), 177.

21. Nolland, *Luke 9:21–18:34*, 646.

22. Lenski states, "As Satan was the general of the wicked angels in this battle, so Michael was the general of the holy angels." Lenski, *Interpretation of St. John's Revelation*, 374. In Matt 25:41, Jesus mirrors this possessive construction.

Jesus's interaction with "Legion" suggests military organization among the demonic ranks. When the Lord asked for a name from the Gerasene demoniac, a spirit responded, "My name is Legion; for we are many" (Mark 5:9).[23] Of course, "legion" describes the demoniac was being thoroughly demonized by a substantial number of entities. But the text's use of singular and plural, "my name" and "we are many," implies that one spirit was probably operating as a representative or leader of the demonic troop. Third, we can also sense a bit of hierarchy in Colossians 1:16 and Ephesians 6:12, but Bruce instructs and cautions us: "In all, five classes of angel-princes seem to be distinguished in the NT – thrones, principalities, authorities, powers, and dominions ... but the variety of ways in which the terms are combined in the NT warns us against any attempt to reconstruct a fixed hierarchy from them."[24]

Additionally, demons can cause different symptoms upon their demonized prey. For instance in Mark 9:25, Jesus cast out a "deaf and mute spirit" that caused its victim to have dangerous seizures.[25] In Luke 13:11–13, Jesus healed a woman whom a demon had bent over and debilitated, freeing her to walk upright again.[26] The Gerasene demoniac of Mark 5 had a host of symptoms, including unnatural strength (5:4) and self-harm (5:5).

But is the word "demons" an overarching term which includes all sorts of beings with differing natures? Are fallen angels and demons the same? The pseudepigraphical book of 1 Enoch, especially in chapters 6–15, narrates how the sons of God or "watchers" perverted humanity through sexual intercourse with human women. Elaborating on Genesis 6, it claims that the offspring of these relationships were giants who died and became evil spirits upon the earth

---

23. According to Guelich, "Legion appears as a Latin loan word. . . . A military term, it designates a unit or brigade in the Roman army including infantry and cavalry. The number varied between 4000 and 6000, but by Jesus' day and during the time of the empire the number appears fixed at approximately 6000 men of whom nearly 5800 were infantry." Guelich, *Mark 1–8:26*, 281.

24. F. F. Bruce, *The Epistles to the Colossians, to Philemon, and to the Ephesians*, New International Commentary on the New Testament (Grand Rapids: Eerdmans, 1984), 63–64.

25. Evans says, "Jesus commands, perhaps ironically, a deaf-mute spirit, and the spirit obeys." Evans, *Mark 8:27–16:20*, 54.

26. While Nolland argues that this is a healing which idiomatically refers to a "spirit," this argument does not seem to fit the language of "having a spirit of infirmity," at least in Luke's usage. Nolland, *Luke 9:21–18:34*, 723–24. Thus we should prefer Stein's explanation: "The woman is described as having an evil spirit that caused her crippled condition." Robert H. Stein, *Luke*, New American Commentary (Nashville: B & H, 1992), 373.

(1 Enoch 15).[27] Thus according to the author of 1 Enoch, corrupt angels and evil spirits are two distinct classes of beings. In other words, fallen angels and demons are ontologically different, since fallen angels are the direct creation of God and demons are the result of illicit angel/human procreation.

Yet 1 Enoch is not Scripture, and much of its contents is dubious at best. The Old Testament includes the existence of giants, but it never affirms that they became demons. They and their descendants died like human beings.[28] Yes, some differences exist between a corrupt son of God in heaven and a demonic being on earth, but the Bible does not indicate a distinction of nature. We would have to carry that argument into the canon.

Despite their distinctions, the demonic host are united in their efforts and activities under the leadership of Satan. When we read of the *shedhim* (protecting spirits translated as demons) in Deuteronomy 32:17, the *bene elohim* (sons of God) of Genesis 6:2, and the *seirim* (goat demons or satyrs) of Leviticus 17:7, we need not think of different beings.[29] Rather they represent the flexibility of the appearances of demons and the expansiveness of their efforts throughout history. We need not declare the demons of the wilderness and the demons of inhabitation as distinct beings, for the story Jesus narrates in Matthew 12:43–45 depicts a single spirit in both circumstances. Nor does 1 Kings 22 furnish a strong distinction between the spirits in heaven and the spirits on earth. In sum, demons are one class of beings with a variety of states, roles, and ranks.

---

27. First Enoch 15 calls these fallen angels "watchers," and Nickelsburg and Baltzer explain,

> By contrast with flesh and blood, the watchers, being spiritual, are immortal and therefore have no need to procreate. Their sin in this case is that they have acted like human beings (thus the conclusion of v 4). They have begotten sons (cf. 6:2) where none were needed, mixing their seed with human blood (cf. Wis 7:2). . . . In [1 Enoch] 15:7b–16:1 the author discusses the results of the watchers' sin, that is, the offspring of the illicit union and their activities. . . . The giants and the spirits that proceed from their dead bodies are spoken of as the same entities. The watchers' willful confusion of the created order has had its inevitable results. Because of their mixed origin . . . these are evil spirits.

Nickelsburg and Baltzer, *1 Enoch*, 272.

28. See 2 Sam 21:18–22 for examples of giants dying as ordinary humans.

29. The *shedhim* (from שֵׁד) refers to a protecting spirit of some kind. Francis Brown, S. R. Driver, and Charles A. Briggs, *A Hebrew and English Lexicon of the Old Testament* (BDB Complete) (Dania Beach, FL: Scribe, *Accordance Electronic Edition*), 993.2. While many modern Bibles translate *seirim* in Lev 17:7 as goat idols, sacrificing to them appears to point to a deeper demonic meaning. These *seirim* (from שָׂעִיר) can refer to goat demons, as Heiser details. Heiser, *Demons*, 24–27.

How Can a Demon and a Human Inhabit the Same Space?

The Bible does not contain a direct answer to the question of how a demon and a human can inhabit the same space. From physics, we can reason that two bodies cannot inhabit the same space. But demons are spirits and function by different parameters, which is illustrated by the biblical testimony that more than one can reside in a human body.[30] So it is not difficult to believe that two spirits, one human and one demonic, could indwell a single human body.

How Do Demons Interact with Humans on a Personal Level?

After looking at the activities and the nature of demons, we can now look at their personhood. Not only does the biblical text describe demons as spiritual beings in contrast to an undefined force, it also describes them as persons. Demons are actors – antagonists – in the redemptive story of Scripture, just as humans are. The Bible includes abstract concepts such as sin and atonement, forces like wind and evil, and other beings like animals. But demons function as persons.

The narratives of Scripture feature many person-to-person interactions between demons and God, holy angels, and humans. From the beginning of Scripture until its final pages, Satan's deceptive intelligence is on display as he converses with Eve and as he argues with the archangel Michael. The demons talk with people and share their unusual knowledge throughout the Gospels, testifying to the heavenly identity of Jesus of Nazareth.

Consider the reference to demons that James makes when criticizing followers of Christ who were arguing about faith and works: "You believe that God is one. You do well; the demons also believe, and shudder" (Jas 2:19).[31] This statement of James supports that humans and demons have a similar capacity

---

30. In addition to the Gerasene demoniac, Jesus also cast multiple demons out of Mary Magdalene, and presumably all were in her at the same time (Luke 8:2).
31. According to Richardson,

> James equated faith without works with mere assent to the truth of God's existence.... Even the demons possess this kind of faith. This claim, perhaps, is an allusion to demons' role as influences in the creation of false religion, what Paul described as "doctrines of demons" (1 Tim 4:10). They could be said to perform miracles and receive worship through the practice of idolatry. James' reference to "demonic faith" can hardly be complimentary. The demons also have monotheistic belief. They know of the reality of God, but they are still malevolent. Many believe that which is true about the Deity, but orthodoxy may have no effect on the evil activities of their lives. The only effect on the demons is that they "shudder" at the thought of God's existence and his power over them.

Richardson, *James*, 134–35.

for belief and intelligence as personal, conscious beings! But the demons' belief is crippled because it is divorced from any holy and happy relationship with God; thus they "shudder" in fear of God and their coming doom. Therefore, unless we begin to manipulate the text, we can see that the Scriptures describe demons as persons who behave in similar ways to human beings; they are real persons and not an impersonal influence or entity.

Another indicator of the personhood of demons is the personal ways they interact with human beings. While many of their behaviors are similar to humans, nothing is as stark as their horrid practice of either oppressing or personally inhabiting individual human beings. Saul, Judas, Mary Magdalene, a slave girl, and the Gerasene demoniac – these and others experienced the horrors of advanced demonization when a wicked spirit neared or entered their body and oppressed, influenced or controlled. And these instances are not merely an unfortunate circumstance or an evil system, but they read like instances where a person afflicts another, like how a child suffers under an evil parent who seizes upon their vulnerabilities. While we do not see visible demons in these encounters, we do see elements of personality. Intelligence, hatred, and intent are present.

The attacks then result in consequences for the affected person, like the abused under the assaults of an abuser. In the case of Saul, the evil spirit's intermittent presence led to terror and rage. "Now the Spirit of the LORD departed from Saul, and an evil spirit from the LORD terrified him" (1 Sam 16:14).[32] This evil spirit also drove Saul to violent madness:

> Now it came about on the next day that an evil spirit from God rushed upon Saul, and he raved in the midst of the house while David was playing the harp with his hand, as usual; and a spear was in Saul's hand. Then Saul hurled the spear, for he thought, "I will pin David to the wall." But David escaped from his presence, twice. (1 Sam 18:10–11)[33]

Satan himself entered Judas to entice and encourage him to betray Jesus (Luke 22:3–4). We can imagine the troubles that the seven spirits caused Mary Magdalene (Mark 16:9). And of course, an evil spirit gave the slave

---

32. Bergen explains, "Saul's tortured state was not an accident of nature, nor was it essentially a medical condition. It was a supernatural assault by a being sent at the Lord's command, and it was brought on by Saul's disobedience." Robert D. Bergen, *1, 2 Samuel*, New American Commentary (Nashville: B & H, 1996), 182.

33. Saul had become like Goliath, threatening the anointed of God. "Like Goliath (cf. 1 Sam 17:7), a previous adversary of David, 'Saul had a spear in his hand.'" Bergen, *1, 2 Samuel*, 201.

girl of Philippi the occult ability to foretell the near future and controlled her movements and speech in following and shouting at Paul (Acts 16:16). This is a person attacking and destroying another. The legion of individual demons in the Gerasene demonic forced him to take off all of his clothes, cut himself, and become extremely strong. Malicious demonic persons cause all of this trouble and destruction.

Conclusion

What is the nature of demons? The many answers in the global context uncover our worldviews and even our agendas. In the church, the worldviews of some are completely contrary to the biblical witness and represent cultural philosophy more than the Scriptures, for example the view of Schleiermacher. Some heighten aspects of demons described in the Scripture to the exclusion of others, like those who insist on the reality of personal demonic beings while ignoring their systematic influence over religions. Others describe demons as systemic evil while downplaying their nature as personal beings. Our cultures are in conflict about the work and nature of demons. The only path to peace and unity is a biblical one.

7

The Corporate Influence of Demons

We have defended the existence of real, personal demonic beings, but we must also acknowledge their collective impact upon human groups. The Bible describes this coordinated malice without diminishing the reality or personality of individual evil spirits. This group work began after the fall of humanity when the entire race became tainted by Adam's sin and Satan's guile. The effects of that demonic deceit are incalculable. But beyond humanity as a whole, what are some other corporate targets of Satan and the demonic host? The Bible highlights four.

Families

The building block of society is the family, and from a strategic standpoint, it is only logical for demons to try to damage the family because the effects of their interference can last for generations. After the fall, we do not have to look far for their efforts in this area. Cain slew his own brother. The first epistle of John explains the situation:

> By this the children of God and the children of the devil are obvious: anyone who does not practice righteousness is not of God, nor the one who does not love his brother.
>
> For this is the message which you have heard from the beginning, that we should love one another; not as Cain, who was of the evil one and murdered his brother. And for what reason did he murder him? Because his own deeds were evil, and his brother's were righteous. (1 John 3:10–12)

According to Akin, "Cain belonged to the evil one, to the devil, a thought that apparently is derived from Gen 4:7, where God warns Cain that 'sin is crouching at your door.' . . . Cain demonstrated the defining actions of his spiritual father (cf. 3:10)."[1] While no recorded dialogue exists between Cain and Satan, John has no trouble tracing Cain's behavior back to the influence of the demonic overlord. This identification does not erase Cain's guilt for his actions, but it does locate the source that fed his malicious desires. To use the biblical phraseology, Cain was a child of the devil, heeding his purposes for the world and for the family. Lutzer provides this summary:

> The Serpent's first attack was against a family and was an attempt to kill a righteous man. The attack was the expression of a religious conflict between two brothers, one of whom could not be content to see the other prosper. Behind the human dynamics was the struggle between God and Satan, between the seed of the woman and the seed of the Serpent.[2]

Demonic attacks against the institution of marriage are also frequent. Paul warns about one form of this attack and explains why sexual abstinence within marriage demands careful regulation. Why? According to 1 Corinthians 7:5, Satan will seize upon our lack of self-control to promote adultery and divorce.[3]

Other cases of demons working to destroy families can be found in the Gospels. We can almost hear the desperation of the demonized persons' relatives. Consider the pleas of this mother in Matthew 15:22: "And a Canaanite woman from that region came out and *began* to cry out, saying, 'Have mercy on me, Lord, Son of David; my daughter is severely demon-possessed.'" And in the Old Testament, one especially brutal instance of satanic involvement to destroy a man and his family is with Job. Satan received the necessary permission from God to trouble Job. But it is still a shock when we read that Job's children were killed during this testing (Job 1:18–19).[4]

---

1. Akin, *1, 2, 3 John*, 155.
2. Lutzer, *God's Devil*, 90.
3. Lenski explains, "Paul would permit and advise only temporary abstinence with a religious background and is very frank in stating the reason, 'on account of your incontinence.' . . . Satan is here pictured as being constantly on the watch to bring Christ's followers to fall. It must be our purpose to thwart his nefarious attempts." R. C. H. Lenski, *The Interpretation of St. Paul's First and Second Epistles to the Corinthians* (Minneapolis: Augsburg, 1963), 279.
4. Alden states, "The first and third calamities were from human enemies. The second and fourth were from natural causes (although all four calamities were caused by the Satan, according to Job 1–2). In v. 16 it was the 'fire of God,' and here it is a 'mighty wind.' The wind came across the desert, indicating the sirocco, a hot sandy wind that blows predominately at the beginning and the end of summer." Alden, *Job*, 60.

Before we move on, we must also address the subject of familial spirits. Are there evil spirits who develop a relationship with a family? With their hostility toward families being well documented, it is plausible, even though the Bible does not directly comment on such familial attachments. Some people claim that dead family members commonly visit them, with or without an occult specialist being involved. The Old Testament prohibitions against necromancy (e.g. Isa 8:9) grant us some clarity here. Arguing that mediums are incapable of contacting human spirits of the departed, Dickason says:

> Some are persuaded that certain mediums can make contact with the spirits of deceased humans. From this they receive comfort and revelation. It results in pride, deception, and bondage to occult powers [i.e. demons]. Consulting with those who had familiar spirits or with wizards was banned in Israel (Lev 19:31; Deut 18:10–11). Corrupt religions about them practiced such things, but Israel would commit apostasy in turning to them.[5]

Evil spirits seem to seize upon our family relationships and exploit them for their own aims. Hence, the Scriptures soundly prohibit necromancy because a non-occult version of consulting the dead does not exist. God has no sanctioned method by which we can contact ancestors and relatives.

As with many demonic strategies and practices, Scripture is otherwise largely silent on the particulars of how demons influence families. The Bible has no need to portray these matters in detail. Instead, we must pursue discretion and discernment, being aware of Satan's schemes and mindful of their many forms in our time. And judging by how corruptive the influence of demons can be in a family, for example that of Adam and Eve, it certainly seems plausible, biblically speaking, that children like Cain and following generations could be haunted, literally or figuratively, by their parent's unlawful forays into the supernatural world.

False Religions

Satan and his servants seek worship. Worship is what Satan tried to win from Jesus in the wilderness temptation (Matt 4:9).[6] As argued previously in chapter

---

5. Dickason, *Angels*, 199.
6. Hagner explains,
    Again the devil tries to detour Jesus away from the will of the Father, offering him something that is within his rights (cf. [Matt] 28:18), but as the following clause shows, at the cost of idolatry. . . . What Jesus received from the magi . . . Satan

4, demons stand behind the various belief systems that oppose the one true God of the Bible. In 1 Corinthians 8 and 10, Paul explains the reality that demons are behind idolatrous religion. They are the "so-called gods" and "lords" whom we are to reject for the Father Creator and Jesus Christ: "For even if there are so-called gods whether in heaven or on earth, as indeed there are many gods and many lords, yet for us there is only one God, the Father, from whom are all things, and we exist for Him; and one Lord, Jesus Christ, by whom are all things, and we exist through Him" (1 Cor 8:5–6).[7]

But in addition to enticing people to accept false beliefs, demons are responsible for promoting the tragic and horrible acts committed in the names of various false religions. One persistent biblical warning is about the religious rite of infant sacrifice. God abhors the practice; it is an abomination to sacrifice a human life to appease false gods.[8] The Scriptures are clear and unflinching on this subject.

> You shall not give any of your children to offer them to Molech, nor shall you profane the name of your God; I am the LORD. (Lev 18:21)[9]

> When the LORD your God cuts off from you the nations which you are going in to dispossess, and you dispossess them and live

---

> desires from Jesus. . . . As in the very first account of testing, failed by Adam and Eve (Gen 3:1–7), the question centers on a choice between the will of Satan or the will of God, which involves implicitly the rendering of worship to the one or the other. Satan indeed vaults himself as god in place of the only God.

Hagner, *Matthew 1–13*, 68.

7. According to Conzelmann,

> In v. 4 he [Paul] acknowledged the rightness of the Corinthians' thesis that the gods do not exist; he merely stated it to be inadequate. Here, on the other hand, he qualifies his concession: there "are" "gods" and "lords." . . . Paul indicates *his* criticism, not only of pagan belief in the gods, but of the gods themselves, first of all by using the word . . . "so-called." They may very well be existent in the sense of being "there" in the world and having a certain power – and Paul himself is convinced that they do exist. But they are not gods. The explanation is provided by Gal 4:8.

Conzelmann, *1 Corinthians*, 143. Emphasis original.

8. While the formal religious expression of this evil is not widespread today, we are still proficient at devaluing the young, discarding them before the idol of self through various abortive practices.

9. Lev 20:1–5 further details God's hatred toward the practice. Mark F. Rooker states, "Support for the interpretation that child sacrifice is what is in view is provided by 2 Kings 23:10 and Jer 7:31. In these texts 'burning' is equated with the expression to cause the children to 'pass through the fire.'" Mark F. Rooker, *Leviticus*, New American Commentary (Nashville: B & H, 2000), 246.

in their land, be careful that you are not ensnared to follow them, after they are destroyed from your presence, and that you do not inquire about their gods, saying, "How do these nations serve their gods, that I also may do likewise?" You shall not behave this way toward the LORD your God, because every abominable act which the LORD hates, they have done for their gods; for they even burn their sons and daughters in the fire to their gods. (Deut 12:29–31)[10]

Furthermore, you took your sons and daughters whom you had borne to Me and sacrificed them to idols to be devoured. Were your obscene practices a trivial matter? You slaughtered My children and offered them to idols by making them to pass through the fire. (Ezek 16:20–21)[11]

And they [Israel] abandoned all the commandments of the LORD their God and made for themselves cast metal images: two calves. And made an Asherah, and worshiped all the heavenly lights, and served Baal. Then they made their sons and their daughters pass through the fire, and practiced divination and interpreting omens, and gave themselves to do evil in the sight of the LORD, provoking Him. (2 Kgs 17:16–17)[12]

These detestable forms of pagan worship were a plague throughout the ancient world. Heider states, "Both classical and patristic writers testify to a cult of child sacrifice, particularly in times of military emergency, in Phoenicia and at Carthage."[13] The locations of child sacrifice were plentiful, as evidenced by the

---

10. Merrill explains:
>To serve other gods is tantamount to aberrant worship, for denial of the uniqueness of the Lord leaves one open to a pluralism of faith and action that knows virtually no limits. To use an extreme example, Moses cited the practice of human sacrifice, a rite exacerbated by the use of one's own children as offerings. Such unspeakable forms of religious expression were common in the ancient Near Eastern world, especially in Canaan, and tragically enough sometimes were emulated by God's own elect nation.

Merrill, *Deuteronomy*, 228.

11. Cooper states, "Children also were sacrificed to pagan gods such as Molech, a practice strictly forbidden in the law. . . . These practices mark a climax of the surrender of the fundamental convictions of the ancient faith of Yahweh in favor of Canaanite heathenism." Cooper, *Ezekiel*, 172.

12. According to House, "They practiced worship rites connected with pagan deities. More specifically, they bowed down before Baal and the Canaanite astral gods. Some of them offered human sacrifices." House, *1, 2 Kings*, 341.

13. G. C. Heider, "Molech," *Dictionary of Deities and Demons*, 582.

archeological excavation of "the remains of children" in various sites in "Sicily, Sardinia, and North Africa."[14] A few people try to slightly soften the biblical texts by saying they describe pagan dedications of babies who became temple prostitutes. "Most scholars, however, remain persuaded that actual sacrifice by fire was involved."[15]

While most would be fine with asserting that such behavior is motivated by demons in some sense, the Scriptures openly declare that sacrifices to false gods are actually to demons. Demons are behind this religiously motivated murder of children.

> They sacrificed to demons who were not God,
> To gods whom they have not known,
> New gods who came lately,
> Whom your fathers did not dread. (Deut 32:17)

> They even sacrificed their sons and their daughters to the demons,
> And shed innocent blood,
> The blood of their sons and their daughters,
> Whom they sacrificed to the idols of Canaan;
> And the land was defiled with the blood. (Ps 106:37–38)[16]

Child sacrifice is an extreme example in Scripture of the influence of demons over religious systems. We should take great care not to imitate the Israelites' duplicity in mixing their beliefs with those of other religious movements and adopting their practices, which is called syncretism. Whether it involves sacrificing humans or simply adopting unbiblical ideas and beliefs, let us reject syncretism and refuse to return to slavery under demonic lords!

The Church

Throughout the New Testament, deceitful spirits aim to pollute and corrupt the church of Jesus Christ. Satan and the demons are the enemy of the church, yet

---

14. Heider, "Molech," 582.
15. Heider, 583.
16. Unger explains these texts and their use of the term "demon." "Demons do exist, first and foremost, for God in His Word says that they exist. That the *shedhim* (Deut. 32:17; Ps. 106:36–37) of the Old Testament were real demons, and not mere idols, is proven by the Septuagint translation of the term by *diamonia* (demons); the Jews regarded idols as demons who allowed themselves to be worshipped by men (Bar. 4:7; LXX Ps. 95:5; 1 Cor. 10:20." Unger, *Biblical Demonology*, 36.

God's people will ultimately prevail in Christ. In the meantime, Satan continues to influence and affect believers through numerous avenues.

The first mode of attack is through false teaching. Paul warns Timothy (and us) that some visible members of the church will fall away, "paying attention to deceitful spirits and teachings of demons" (1 Tim 4:1).[17] Demonic spirits spread their lies through the "hypocrisy of liars" (1 Tim 4:2) and false prophets. According to Lea and Griffin,

> Paul described the false teachers who practiced misleading the Ephesians. It was these false teachers whom the demons were using to carry out their bidding. First, Paul pictured their treachery by denouncing them as hypocrites. They presented themselves as pious followers of Christ, but they were in reality glib tools of the devil.[18]

First John describes how false prophets are connected to deceitful spirits: "Beloved, do not believe every spirit, but test the spirits to see whether they are from God, because many false prophets have gone out into the world" (1 John 4:1). Strecker and Attridge say:

> The author [of 1 John] takes for granted the existence of a variety of spirits. In what follows it will be apparent that this multiplicity of *pneumata* is at work especially in the preaching of the false prophets.... Thus the community is warned not to submit itself to the various spirits, but to maintain a critical distance from them, that is, to 'test' them. The purpose of this testing is to determine "whether they are from God.".... This was the common attitude of the primitive Christian church, in its earliest days, toward "heresy."[19]

Thus, the variety of ideas and doctrines that fall under the banner of Christianity are not entirely the result of human disagreements or diversity. Corruptive and deceptive contributions are added by demons who strive to disintegrate the biblical cohesion of the universal church.

---

17. Lea and Griffin state, "Paul's concluding statement of v. 1 located the source of the deceitful teachings in demonic influence. Satan's ability to enlist Judas to do his will shows his competence to influence belief and behavior (Luke 22:3)." Lea and Griffin, *1, 2 Timothy, Titus*, 128.

18. Lea and Griffin, 128.

19. Strecker and Attridge, *The Johannine Letters*, 133.

The second way that demons harass the church is by temptation and the promotion of immorality. One prominent form of temptation is through affliction. In 1 Thessalonians 3:5, Satan is called the "tempter." But how were the Thessalonians tempted? Satan hindered their development by obstructing their ability to fellowship with Paul (1 Thess 2:17–3:3). Paul's fear was that Satan might succeed in tempting them to abandon the truth. He sent Timothy to ensure that they would remain "faith-ful" in that "faith."[20] Affliction was in fact a temptation wielded by the tempter. And in chapter 4, we discussed demons' attempts to undermine healthy biblical rules for sexuality through temptation. They prey on our human desires. And as they promote false doctrines and false shepherds as leaders over the Lord's sheep, it inevitably leads to sinful abuse by these leaders, along with wickedness (such as sexual sin) among the flock members. In this effort of the enemy, all are vulnerable, but the issue of church leadership and new converts deserves special attention. That elders, pastors, and other leaders be spiritually mature and have honorable reputations are non-negotiable, as Paul states when giving the standards for elder selection. Paul urges Timothy to choose someone who is "not a new convert, so that he will not become conceited and fall into condemnation incurred by the devil. And he must have a good reputation with those outside the church, so that he will not fall into disgrace and the snare of the devil" (1 Tim 3:6–7). New converts in particular "are more vulnerable to the schemes of the devil," and so should not be put "into positions of leadership."[21] Satan and his demonic host work hard to trap leaders and pollute the church so they can compromise its witness and mission to the world.

A third way that demons work to destroy the church is by creating and encouraging division. Writing to the tumultuous congregation of Corinth, Paul voices his concerns as he attempts to bring about reconciliation and forgiveness. "But one whom you forgive anything, I also forgive; for indeed what I have forgiven, if I have forgiven anything, I did so for your sakes in the presence of Christ, so that no advantage would be taken of us by Satan, for we are not ignorant of his schemes" (2 Cor 2:10–11).[22] When Satan assails the church through his many schemes, in this case to divide and destroy through a lack of

---

20. Fee, *The First and Second Letters to the Thessalonians*, 116.

21. Philip H. Towner, *The Letters to Timothy and Titus*, New International Commentary on the New Testament (Grand Rapids: Eerdmans, 2006), 258.

22. According to Lenski, "[Satan] hoped to frustrate the whole blessed work that had been done in Corinth and to deliver a stunning blow to Paul. These evil results would spread to even other congregations." Lenski, *Interpretation of St. Paul's First and Second Epistles to the Corinthians*, 891.

forgiveness, the best defense is to stand united. As Garland states on this text, "Satan is powerless before a united community filled with love and humble forgiveness."[23] Demons are enemies of reconciliation, and "Satan fans the flames of hurt into an inferno of hostility."[24] The church may be an earthly safehouse from the rule of Satan, but it is not excluded from his influential schemes.

Finally, the sovereign purposes of God to instruct believers mysteriously work in and through demonic actions against the church. Demons serve as a tool of God's discipline of his people. Some Pauline passages discuss this concept that God's purposes in the church and her members prevail paradoxically through Satan's work.

> I [Paul] have decided to turn such a [unrepentant] person over to Satan for the destruction of his body, so that his spirit may be saved in the day of the Lord. (1 Cor 5:5)[25]

> Because of the extraordinary greatness of the revelations, for this reason, to keep me [Paul] from exalting myself, there was given me a thorn in the flesh, a messenger of Satan to torment me – to keep me from exalting myself! (2 Cor 12:7)[26]

> Keeping faith and a good conscience, which some have rejected and suffered shipwreck in regard to their faith. Among these are Hymenaeus and Alexander, whom I [Paul] have handed over to Satan, so that they will be taught not to blaspheme. (1 Tim 1:19–20)[27]

---

23. Garland, *2 Corinthians*, 131–32.
24. Garland, 132.
25. Mark Taylor explains,
    The meaning in 1 Cor 5:5 would be to excommunicate the offender from the community in order to destroy his sinful orientation so that he himself might be saved on the Day of the Lord. This interpretation assumes that Paul is speaking primarily of the individual. Paul is equally concerned, however, for the sanctity of the church, which is expressed in the analogy that follows of the leaven that infects the whole batch of dough (5:6–8).
    Mark Taylor, *1 Corinthians*, New American Commentary (Nashville: B & H, 2014), 137.
26. Garland states, "God permits Satan to strike the apostle, but God turns the stricken Paul into an even greater instrument of his power. A proud, arrogant Paul would have only hindered the gospel's advance. A humiliated, frail Paul, led as a captive in God's triumph, has accelerated the gospel's progress so that the fragrance of knowing God spreads everywhere." Garland, *2 Corinthians*, 522.
27. According to Lea and Griffin, "The purpose of handing them over to Satan was not merely punitive but chiefly corrective or formative in purpose. By excluding them from the fellowship of God's people, Paul hoped that Satan's affliction of the troublemakers would teach them not to insult the Lord by their words and deeds." Lea and Griffin, *1, 2 Timothy, Titus*, 81.

We should not conceptualize that Satan is waiting outside the front door of a church building, ready to receive and torment the excommunicated. Rather, the wording in 1 Corinthians 5:5 "means to turn him back out into Satan's sphere," expelling the unrepentant one from the church.[28] This practice leads to discipline, since the person will be removed from the blessings of the church and experience only the dominion of Satan. Thus in 1 Timothy 1:20, Paul "handed over" Hymenaeus and Alexander. Satan, through all of his minions and activities in the world, is "seen as serving God's purposes by overseeing the chastisement of sinners" removed from the body of Christ.[29] God uses Satan's wickedness to provoke his own people to repentance and purity.

Outside the body of Christ is the domain of demons under their fiendish leader, Satan. The deception, death, and destruction of the world systems is evident to the members of the church, for they know the death they have escaped and the life they have entered. Yet God's people still crave the sinfulness of the age! By turning the unrepentant back into the demonic realm of the world, the hope is that Satan's work will function as discipline, jolting the wayward to wakefulness.

Paul's personal experience with Satanically driven discipline presents another consideration. While still under the broader category of discipline, the experience is not about chastening the unrepentant but about preventing sin, specifically pride in Paul's life. God gives a "thorn" to Paul, defined as a "messenger" or "angel" from the evil one (2 Cor 12:7). Whether this directly refers to a demon or indirectly means "something bad under Satan's dominion" is beside the point. Like that of Job, "God is the invisible source of this suffering in the life of Paul," and Satan's involvement furthers God's purposes for Paul.[30] Paul's suffering thereby protects the fledgling church from the potential devastation of immoral leadership. God sovereignly coordinates all circumstances and persons, including the demonic powers and their actions, for his glory and the good of his church – disciplining the unrepentant and discouraging sins like pride.

---

28. Gordon D. Fee, *The First Epistle to the Corinthians*, New International Commentary on the New Testament (Grand Rapids: Eerdmans, 2014), 229.

29. Towner, *Letters to Timothy and Titus*, 161.

30. Paul Barnett, *The Second Epistle to the Corinthians*, New International Commentary on the New Testament (Grand Rapids: Eerdmans, 1997), 570.

Politics

Since the Scriptures label the spiritual beings as "rulers" (Eph 6:12), it logically follows that they intervene in the political affairs of the nations. Scripture recounts a couple of instances of demon influence in the nation of Israel. As we discussed earlier, an evil spirit harassed the first king, Saul. Yet even when his far superior successor, David, ascended to the throne, 1 Chronicles 21:1 curiously records that Satan (or an adversary who was possibly the angel of the Lord) "incited David to count Israel," leading to devastating national consequences.

Daniel 10 is a crucial text for analyzing the angels and demons that operate behind political movements and rule countries. Scripture identifies them as "princes" and associates them with their assigned peoples. In Daniel 10:21, Michael is identified as a prince of Israel, and he and the angel Gabriel fight against the demon prince of Persia who tried to stop Gabriel from delivering his message to Daniel (10:13).

> Then he [the angel Gabriel] said, "Do you understand why I came to you? But I shall now return to fight against the prince of Persia; so I am leaving, and behold, the prince of Greece is about to come. However, I will tell you what is recorded in the writing of truth. Yet there is no one who stands firmly with me against these forces except Michael your prince." (Dan 10:20–21)[31]

Stephen Miller comments on this unusual passage:

> The angel added that later "the prince of Greece will come," implying that he would fight against this prince also. In keeping with the identification of the previously mentioned prince of Persia, "the prince of Greece" would be Satan or one of his demons. This evil spirit would come later when the empire of Greece rose to power, indicating that the angelic conflict would continue into the time of the Greek Empire.[32]

The following chapter of Daniel then prophetically details the political struggles that would come. The link is straightforward in chapters 10 and 11: The actions of supernatural beings influenced the political environment that would impact the present and future of Israel.

---

31. The translators of the NASB helpfully furnish "Satanic angel" as the implied meaning for the opposing princes.
32. Stephen R. Miller, *Daniel*, New American Commentary (Nashville: B & H, 1994), 288.

We can also tease out the impact of demons on politics from other texts as well. In the temptation of Christ in Matthew 4:8–9, Satan offers "all the kingdoms of the world" to Jesus in exchange for worship, implying that he has supremacy over them. This offer was not an empty one. Revelation 20:1–3 describes how Satan is captured by Jesus and stripped of his deceptive power over the nations, though he briefly attempts a foolhardy rebellion (20:7–10). According to the Scriptures, demons influence not only individuals but also nations.

In the previous chapters, we surveyed the biblical content concerning Satan and demons. We prioritized their activity and speech, since the Bible focuses primarily on their behavior. Building on that material, we then analyzed their nature as literal, personal beings. We also highlighted their influence on individuals and on families, false religions, the church, and politics. But why does this all matter for us? Let us now focus on the purpose of this demonology.

8

The Purpose of a Demonology for the Global Church

At the beginning of this work we asked a question. It befits us to repeat it again. "Why demonology?" Then we quickly assessed how living in this world and reading the Bible presents the question as unavoidable. In one sense, we all answer this question with varying degrees of understanding and accuracy.

We have arrived at a juncture where we have reviewed the biblical texts concerning the demonic. We have done some demonological study, but we have yet to show exactly how it affects us. Biblical demonology has a purpose, and we are not to remain unchanged. With all of this in mind, let us address four realms in which demonology carries weight, fields that our demonological efforts should assist and inform.

Biblical Reliability

Does the Bible mean what it says? Scholars and commentators repeatedly confirm that the Scriptures depict a cosmos populated with demonic beings who interact with humans. But then we often try to temper the impact of that news! Our perspective of demonology reveals our bibliology. We must ask ourselves, does the Bible reliably portray the demonic? Does it depict the facts about the supernatural world, realities that are still true today? If the biblical witnesses concerning the demonic are merely myths that have no bearing on reality, what else in Scripture is a fable? This is a slippery slope, and demonology is an easy place to begin the slide, especially for the post-Enlightenment Western mind. Giant issues hang upon these related doctrines of demonology.

Is all of this reflection trivial? If we give over the demonic as we have portrayed it to the rubbish heap of history, perhaps it is no huge loss if one Christian believes demons to be mythical while another believes in their reality? Unger vigorously exposes the true dangers that lurk in the anti-supernatural redefinition of the demonic.

> There is not a hint that Jesus or any of the New Testament writers had the slightest doubt as to the real existence of either Satan or demons. . . . Only slight investigation is necessary to expose the extreme crudity, destructiveness, and untenability of the rationalistic and mythical view of Satan and demons. It not only jeopardizes the character and truthfulness of the Son of God himself, but challenges the authenticity and reliability of the whole Bible. For if the teachings of Scripture on the subject of Satan and demons are judged mythical, any other doctrine of Holy Writ may likewise be declared mythical at the caprice of the critic, who is disposed to offset his opinions against those of the prophets, apostles, and the Lord Himself.[1]

Unger's comprehensive remarks from 1952 leave little room for improvement decades later. We lose much if we unceremoniously transform biblical demons into fantasies, moral tools, or symbols. In this arena of study and many others, an interpreter's opinion, culture, or philosophy can slant and misrepresent the Scripture's intention. Thus, the biblical demonology we endorse serves to uphold biblical reliability.

Soteriological Quality

How does demonology serve the doctrine of salvation, or soteriology? Before we advance any further, we must quickly define the parameters of the soteriological field from an evangelical perspective. After a substantial overview of the subject of salvation, R. E. O. White in the *Evangelical Dictionary of Theology* states, "It is evident, even from this brief outline, that need would arise for endless analysis, comparison, systematization, and restatement in contemporary terms of all that salvation means to the Christian faith. This is the task of soteriology, the doctrine of *soteria* – salvation."[2] But what does salvation and soteriology

---

1. Unger, *Biblical Demonology*, 36–37.
2. R. E. O. White, "Salvation," in *Evangelical Dictionary of Theology*, ed. Walter A. Elwell (Grand Rapids: Baker Book House, 1984), 969.

encompass? White demonstrates some of the comprehensiveness of salvation with this list of various aspects:

> religious (acceptance with God, forgiveness, reconciliation, sonship, reception of the Spirit, immortality); emotional (strong assurance, peace, courage, hopefulness, joy); practical (prayer, guidance, discipline, dedication, service); personal (new thoughts, convictions, horizons, motives, satisfactions, self-fulfillment); social (new sense of community with Christians, of compassion toward all, overriding impulse to love as Jesus has loved).[3]

Of course, this definition of salvation means little if we do not remember from what we have been saved – "sin and death; guilt and estrangement; ignorance of truth; bondage to habit and vice; fear of demons, of death, of life, of God, of hell; despair of self; alienation from others; pressures of the world; a meaningless life."[4]

Unfortunately, White's discussion of the nature of salvation and soteriology does not include much else on our deliverance from Satan and his demonic powers.[5] Paul Enns in *The Moody Handbook of Theology* does briefly state that Christ "defeated Satan, rendering him impotent in the believer's life. Satan had the power of death over people, but that power was broken through Christ (Heb. 2:14)."[6] Thankfully, other academics like Ferdinando attempt to remedy the evangelical scholarly community's lack of materials on this subject.

Let us turn to Ferdinando's *The Triumph of Christ in African Perspective* in which he specifically details the demonological aspect of redemption. Under a section entitled "Redemption and Evil Supernatural Beings," Ferdinando states, "The notion of Satan's defeat and of the liberation of his victims is clearly included among the New Testament concepts of redemption. Its Old Testament background is found in the figure of the divine warrior redeeming his oppressed people by the conquest of their foes (Exod. 15:1ff.)."[7]

---

3. White, "Salvation," 968.
4. White, 968.
5. Sadly, this brief treatment of demonology in soteriology in an evangelical reference work is not unusual, especially in the West. For instance, Wayne Grudem's famous book *Systematic Theology: An Introduction to Biblical Doctrine* has twelve chapters on the doctrine of the application of redemption, but none target our liberation from demonic powers. The demonic is primarily under the doctrine of God, which includes God's creation and works.
6. Paul Enns, *Moody Handbook of Theology* (Chicago: Moody, 2014), 308.
7. Ferdinando, *Triumph of Christ*, 365.

Redemption and soteriology include deliverance from the demonic, and Ferdinando explains our salvation from Satan's power using several biblical themes for support. First, he points us toward Christ's exorcisms:

> In the synoptic gospels Jesus' exorcisms identify him as the one who brings in the kingdom of God, liberating those oppressed by Satan (Mat. 12:28–29; Mk. 3:27; Lk. 11:20–22; cf. Acts 10:38; Lk. 13:16) and bringing the oppressor's power to an end (Lk. 10:18; Matt. 4:8 & 28:18ff.). However, while the exorcisms, like the healings, show that the kingdom has come in that people are being freed from every sort of affliction, in none of the synoptic gospels do they constitute its substance.... It is not the destruction of demonic activity by overwhelming force that Jesus has primarily come to achieve (cf. Matt. 8:29), but the liberation of Satan's victims from the real, moral source of their enslavement.[8]

And Ferdinando also gives the soteriological implications of demonology when he discusses the cross, stating, "Other New Testament writers however do indicate a relationship between Jesus' death and evil supernatural beings, the Johannine writings and Hebrews having Satan particularly in view, the Pauline epistles and 1 Peter the 'powers.'"[9] Ferdinando argues that "there are hints of the divine warrior."[10] But he remains steadfast in refusing to remove sin from the heart of the equation. "Thus the object of Christ's death was not primarily the defeat of Satan or of the powers, but the rescue of their victims from their own disobedience and its consequences."[11] The reasons for which Satan accused us were undone by the Christ who bore our sin! Ferdinando completes this theme at its eschatological resolution:

> In their demonology the New Testament writers demonstrate the same eschatological tension which characterizes their understanding of salvation. Satan and the powers are defeated yet remain active while they await final judgment.... Moreover there is some suggestion that the same Christ who triumphed over them by his death will also crush them in the climactic act of salvation and judgment (1 Cor. 15:25; Rev. 19:11ff.). The present period between Satan's two judgments is characterized by

---

8. Ferdinando, 366.
9. Ferdinando, 366.
10. Ferdinando, 366.
11. Ferdinando, 366.

a tension between Christ's reign and Satan's hostility towards the church.... [Jesus'] reign assures his people of both the security of their salvation and the availability of divine resources in their conflict against hostile powers.[12]

Our Savior delivered the demonized and defeated our spiritual enemies with his own death. He is continuing to save, protect, and equip his people, aware of the devious and destructive powers who assault the church. This soteriological mission will endure until Christ permanently casts Satan and his host into the lake of fire. Ferdinando rightly unfolds this net of doctrines where soteriology and demonology intersect. His work covers the omissions of the *Evangelical Dictionary of Theology* and other materials. Thus, in possession of a more rigorous definition of soteriology, let us more deeply assess how demonology supports the quality of the Christian doctrine of salvation.

How exactly does our demonology realign our soteriology? Yes, we affirm Jesus's penal substitutionary death on the cross, propitiating the Father's wrath against sin and sinners, but a biblically refreshed demonology challenges us to elaborate on the predominantly demon-less soteriology found in many Protestant formulations. What specifically demands reevaluation? Let us consider that question under three primary branches.

The first branch is that from which we are saved. Recognizing the domination and rule of the world by false gods, our soteriology requires redesigning. We not only live in a sinful world; we inhabit a realm of demonic powers. "And even if our gospel is veiled, it is veiled to those who are perishing, the god of this world has blinded the minds of the unbelieving so that they might not see the light of the gospel of the glory of Christ, who is the image of God" (2 Cor 4:3–4).[13] Satan snatches away the truth, according to the parable in Mark's gospel (Mark 4:15).[14] Satan and his affiliates orchestrate the idolatry and false religious systems that organize and saturate the nations.

This matter raises a question. How do we transfer from the dominion of the devil to the kingdom of God in Christ? The Scriptures state that such

---

12. Ferdinando, 367–68.

13. Garland states, "Paul must be referring to Satan as the god of this age. He classifies Satan as a 'god' because he has a dominion, however limited by the one true God, and has subjects whom Paul labels 'unbelievers.'" Garland, *2 Corinthians*, 211.

14. According to Lenski, "Through the ears the Word 'has been sown into them,' and ... is now lying in the minds of these hearers but does not stay there to do its blessed work. Satan, moved by his inordinate wickedness and opposition to God, snatches the sown Word away from these hearers." R. C. H. Lenski, *The Interpretation of St. Mark's Gospel* (Minneapolis: Augsburg, 1961), 172.

a transfer takes place, which Paul explains in Colossians 1:13–14, "For He rescued us from the domain of darkness, and transferred us to the kingdom of His beloved Son, in whom we have redemption, the forgiveness of sins."[15] As a preacher of the gospel of Jesus, Paul received a command "to open their eyes so that they may turn from darkness to light, and from the power of Satan to God" (Acts 26:18). Commenting on these texts from Colossians and Acts, Melick declares, "In Christ, God invaded Satan's territory and delivered people."[16] Two kingdoms exist, and believing Christ's gospel is the exclusive remedy for deliverance from Satan's power.

Christ accomplished all of this by the cross, paying the penalty for sin! Who can bring a charge against the justified in Christ? As described in Colossians 2 and Galatians 4, our full and final redemption in Jesus Christ has loosed us from the chains of the rules and regulations by which the demonic powers manipulate and enslave humanity.

The second branch is how we are being saved. Our ongoing sanctification and growth in godliness are not merely a battle against our sinful desires and the corporate patterns of our age. Throughout our daily lives as followers of Christ and members of his kingdom, we are warring with demonic powers on the personal, familial, corporate, and national levels. In Ephesians 6, Paul explains how we must put on the equipment – the armor of God – for such a conflict with "spiritual forces of wickedness in the heavenly places" (Eph 6:12). In keeping with the instructions in Ephesians 4–5, we are therefore urged in Ephesians 6:14–20 to battle primarily through holy and obedient living, resting on the resources secured through the cross in Christ – righteousness, truth, peace, faith, salvation, the Spirit, and access to God in prayer.[17] As the yeast of the kingdom of God is kneaded into this world through evangelism and missions, to borrow imagery from Jesus's parable in Matthew 13:33, the global church increasingly exposes Satan and the other demonic powers as false gods – no gods – with laws and practices that only enslave.

---

15. Lenski explains, "To the Father's making us fit, rescuing, and transferring us there is now added what has been bestowed upon us sinners to make us fit for the kingdom of the Son: 'in connection with whom (faith making this connection) we have the ransoming, the forgiveness of sins' which once held us bound under the authority of the darkness." Lenski, *The Interpretation of St. Paul's Epistles to the Colossians, to the Thessalonians, to Timothy, to Titus and to Philemon*, 43.

16. Melick, *Philippians, Colossians, Philemon*, 207.

17. In one sense, through union with him, Christ is our armor – our Righteousness, Truth, Peace, Gospel, Salvation, Faith, and Word!

The third branch is how we will be saved – eschatological soteriology. Our proposed demonology reminds us that this aspect of salvation must also be well-rounded. Ultimately, the kingdom of God and its King will come. Christ will throw down every evil power, and the true Lord will establish his dominion, vindicate his right to rule, and unseat the cruel spiritual masters of this world. By his grace and with Christ, we will crush Satan (Rom 16:20), fulfilling the *proto-evangelium*.[18] Thus, salvation from first to last only has its proper form when we partner it with a robust demonology.

However, in the doctrine of salvation, one issue merits a thorough examination in relation to the doctrine of the demonic. Throughout the world, universalism, syncretism, and inclusivism are pervasive.[19] Our pluralistic age challenges the Christian message. Who is saved? Do multiple ways to God exist? Does salvation exist outside of Christianity, and can traditional religions and other forms of general revelation assist in salvation, empower the process, or even accomplish the task? Speaking from his African context, Kato's summary of demonic activity to influence worldly thinking is helpful:

> But the devil has many other avenues for fighting against Christ and His church and he knows where best to succeed. Christo-paganism appears to be the area of attack within the next generation. . . . The unique claims of Christ are regarded as eccentricities. The relativity philosophy is seeking to make the Scriptures only one of many revelations rather than a special revelation. Christianity is not repudiated but is given the largest room in the camp of religions. It is claimed that the difference lies not in kind but in qualitative teachings. "Thus saith the Lord" as a prepositional revelation is reduced to merely a segment of general revelation or a fulfillment of other revelations. By this process it cannot dislodge other revelations but only improve upon them. That being the case, salvation is no monopoly of Christianity. It is just as possible to be saved through other religions as it is

---

18. The *proto-evangelium* refers to the "first gospel," the first good news, that the seed of the woman would crush the serpent (Gen 3:15).

19. We previously defined syncretism as the mixing of competing and contrary religious ideas, but we should also mention inclusivism and universalism. The term "inclusivism" refers to the unbiblical idea that some people who do not follow and trust in Christ will be included in Christ's work of redemption and ultimately saved. This position leaves room in heaven for the so-called "holy lost," those who are devout in their pursuit of the divine in other religions but die apart from Christ. Universalism is the idea that all persons who have ever existed, regardless of their disposition toward Jesus, will be redeemed and saved.

through Christianity though the latter may bring salvation faster. Such is the kind of thought prevailing today. These are theological pitfalls that only a discerning, Spirit-filled Bible-believer can see and refute.[20]

Kato upholds a strict exclusivism; only Christians, authentic followers of Jesus who transcend mere nominal or consumeristic "christianities," are the recipients of salvation. As for all other competitors, "non-Christian religions prove man has a concept of God but they also show man's rebellion against God (Rom. 1:18–23)."[21] Kato emphasizes that Christ is unique, and his ministry is unmatched. "God has redemptively become incarnate in Christ for the redemption of mankind, but only those who accept His offer of salvation can be saved."[22]

Biblical demonology underscores this exclusivism while rejecting any inclusivist and universalist notions within soteriology. Undermining Christianity's exclusivity is Satan's strategy for retaining his dominion over those in sin. This satanic tactic also makes it harder for freedom-preaching evangelists to be heard. Consider 1 John 5:18–19: "We know that no one who is born of God sins; but He who was born of God keeps him, and the evil one does not touch him. We know that we are of God, and that the whole world lies in the power of the evil one."[23] The Bible portrays a world in moral, spiritual, and religious bondage – under the oppression of a manipulative and destructive overlord. From an exclusivist viewpoint, only the gospel of Jesus Christ delivers people from this predicament.

But is that what the biblical author of 1 John intended to convey? The immediate contextual question is "How is one born of God?" and the author answers our query in 1 John 5:1a, "Everyone who believes that Jesus is the Christ has been born of God." Strecker and Attridge remark on this passage:

> The address is to every Christian, for it is true of all of them that they believe that Jesus is the Christ. Hence nothing is said here directly against any opponents. They are only indirectly in view, to

---

20. Kato, *Theological Pitfalls in Africa*, 173–74.
21. Kato, 181.
22. Kato, 182.
23. Lenski comments that this text means that the world "lies prostrate in [the devil's] power domain." R. C. H. Lenski, *The Interpretation of the Epistles of St. Peter, St. John and St. Jude* (Minneapolis: Augsburg, 1966), 539. Also, this text can give the false impression that the "born of God" are perfect, without error. Rather, context like 1 John 1:10 leads us to read "No one who is born of God is (actively, continually) sinning."

> the extent that they deny that Jesus is the Christ. . . . [the address] confesses Jesus as the Christ and articulates its credo, that is, the *fides quae creditur* ("that which is believed") (cf. 4:15). . . . This attitude of trust is founded on the fact of being born of God, which is the sign by which Christians are known, and which as early as 4:7 was equated with love and with knowing God.[24]

Trust in Christ, or lack thereof, is the defining factor as to whether or not one is born of God.

This doctrine then carries down into our reading of 1 John 5:18–19. Again, we return to the thoughts of Strecker and Attridge on this text.

> If [Jesus Christ] protects the people who are born of God, the complete thought would be: what is primary for those born of God is their relationship to God. They are "protected" from the evil one by Christ (v. 18). They are thereby separated from the world (v. 19) and have knowledge of the "true God" (v. 20). When Christians know that they are secure under the rule of Christ, they are withdrawn from the sphere of the devil's power. The "evil one" cannot touch them to stain them with sin. . . .
>
> It is on the basis of "being from God" that humans can be preserved from the power of the evil one, for such existence is at the same time a matter of being defined by the one who was born of God, that is, Christ. . . . In v. 19 the dualistic contrast contained in the preceding verse is taken up and interpreted. The difference between God and the devil here corresponds to the alternative between God and the world. When believers are grounded in God they are separated from the world, which "lies under the power of the evil one." This separation is then recognized through faith, with a knowledge that can only be achieved in faith.[25]

Let us summarize the points of this argument: (1) Those who believe in Jesus as the Messiah are born of God. (2) Those who are born of God are protected from the evil one. (3) A two-party distinction exists in 1 John 5. Those who are born of God by faith in Jesus are with God, and those who are not, "the whole world" (v. 19), are under the power of evil one. If we accept 1 John 5, we should therefore acknowledge an exclusivist viewpoint and compassionately seek to evangelize those whom the god of this world has blinded.

---

24. Strecker and Attridge, *Johannine Letters*, 175.
25. Strecker and Attridge, 209.

The intersection of demonology and exclusivism is persistent throughout the Scriptures. Consider another example, 2 Corinthians 6:14–15, which highlights the divide between the saved and unsaved, those with Christ and those with "Belial." The parties are unsuitable for unity as members of God's family: "Do not be mismatched with unbelievers; for what do righteousness and lawlessness share together, or what does light have in common with darkness? Or what harmony does Christ have with Belial ['worthless one,' Satan], or what does a believer share with an unbeliever?"[26] What is the intended meaning of these verses? Garland states:

> Paul has in mind an alliance with spiritual opposites, and the image of harnessing oneself to someone who is spiritually incompatible evokes images of spiritual disaster. . . . The contrasts in this verse between light and darkness, Christ and Belial, are rooted in Paul's conviction, stated in [2 Cor] 4:4, that "The God of this age has blinded the minds of unbelievers, so that they cannot see the light of the gospel of the glory of Christ, who is the image of God." The God of this world (Belial) only spreads darkness by blinding people. Consequently, there can be no harmony between Christ, who is light, and dark Belial. . . . In 1 Cor 10:20 he warns them that participating in pagan feasts is to share in the worship of demons. Christ and demons do not belong at the same table.[27]

Paul is telling the Corinthian Christians to be holy and separate in a pagan society. The danger persists that many Christians are joined with unbelievers in idolatrous and sinful causes. Such unions show allegiances with the wrong parties rather than to Christ. Paul leaves no room for middle ground. The pagan world rejects Jesus, in whole or in part, and dwells in darkness. And all allegiances are to one of two personalities, two lords – Jesus or Belial (Satan).

Thus, interfaith and ecumenical cooperation should only progress so far, in that we find commonality in some efforts to seek the welfare of our neighbors. But we cannot go so far as to obscure the divide between the salvation in Christ and the lostness of false religion under Satan. For we can only find true, complete unity in Christ. Salvation is through Jesus Christ, outside of

---

26. According to Garland, "Belial is a Hebrew word . . . that may mean 'worthlessness' (see 1 Sam 25:25), 'ruin,' or 'wickedness.' In the intertestamental period it was used as a name for Satan, much as Lucifer was once a popular name for Satan in English. . . . Paul possibly chose the term Belial because he wanted a personal name as the antithesis of Christ." Garland, *2 Corinthians*, 335.

27. Garland, 331.

the domain of Satan, and the division between those who believe in Jesus Christ alone and those who do not is pronounced.[28] Sadly, it is no surprise that inclusivism and universalism are flourishing across the world within Christianity, in step with the embrace of substandard, cultural perspectives of the demonic!

We would be remiss to neglect an admonition. Upholding exclusivism should not produce arrogance. Instead, exclusivism and a correct understanding of the demonic should encourage compassion for those who do not hold the same view. Our references to demons may sound like strong, combative language. But we should not attack the unconverted, those who unwittingly languish under the dominion of Satan and his minions, with military rhetoric. Rather, the church's motivation and empowerment for evangelism and missions should be compassion. When Jesus evangelized the crowds, healed the sick, delivered the demonized, and faced accusations of being demonized himself, he showed this compassion.

> Jesus was going through all the cities and villages, teaching in their synagogues and proclaiming the gospel of the kingdom, and healing every kind of disease and every sickness.
> Seeing the crowds, He felt compassion for them, because they were distressed and downcast, like sheep without a shepherd. Then

---

28. Borchert inserts an extraordinary rebuke of modern pluralism in his commentary on John 14:6.

> Here John joins three powerful ideas of "way," "truth," and "life" to produce a classic statement concerning the significance of Jesus in providing salvation. . . .
> The concepts of these three terms are rooted solidly in the teaching of the Old Testament and in Hebrew thought. . . . For example, the Psalmist prays that the Lord would teach him the divine "way" and lead him to walk in "truth" (Ps 84:11), and he contemplates the "path of life" (Ps 16:11) as his blessed hope. . . .
> Moreover, here at 14:6 John follows the lead of the Prologue, where he already had asserted strongly that no one else has ever seen God, but the only Son has made him known (1:18). Now in this verse John concludes with an emphatic assertion ["No one comes to the Father except through me"]. . . . Any hint at universalism, syncretistic patterns of salvation, or reaching the Father through any other means than Jesus is here completely eliminated.
> The issue of Johannine exclusivism is therefore placed squarely before the reader. Given the fact that the Johannine church was a community struggling for its existence in the midst of powerful pressures from both its Jewish birthing setting and its Hellenistic syncretistic context, the language and antisociety stance may seem to be completely out of touch with today's adoption of pluralism. . . .
> The Johannine concept of mission is uncompromising on the issue of the uniqueness of Jesus. For this assertion they were willing to die or be excluded from the synagogues in the pattern of the blind man (9:34).

Gerald L. Borchert, *John 12-21*, New American Commentary (Nashville: B & H, 2002), 108–111.

He said to His disciples, "The harvest is plentiful, but the workers are few. Therefore plead with the Lord of the harvest to send out workers into His harvest." (Matt 9:35–38)[29]

Craig Blomberg describes the missional attitude of Jesus: "Despite Jesus' extensive ministry, many in Israel, no doubt even in Galilee, remain unreached with his message. Jesus' human emotions reflect a deep, *gut level* 'compassion' . . . for this sea of humanity."[30] The religious and national leadership had failed the masses, which prompted Jesus to show compassion.

Soteriology, we discover, is broad in scope and content, including both what we are redeemed *from* and what we are saved *to*. Thanks to biblical demonology, we can view a fuller and clearer picture of salvation. Through the redemptive work of Jesus Christ, we experience deliverance from the power and dominion of Satan and his associates.

Practical Ministry

Demonology is not a mere academic exercise. The biblical texts on the demonic require organization into a systematic doctrine, but that doctrine is not without pastoral purpose. While this study is not a spiritual warfare guide, the study of demonology is practical. Here are four areas where demonology strengthens Christian ministry.

First, demonology prepares us to defend not merely against impersonal principles or forces but against literal, personal, evil beings. Defending the biblical material about demons, John Calvin remarks, "We must here likewise refute those who foolishly allege that devils are nothing but bad affections or perturbations suggested by our carnal nature. . . . The subject, however, deserved to be touched upon, lest any, by embracing that error, should imagine they have no enemy, and thereby be more remiss or less cautious in resisting."[31] Calvin's point is that the dismissal and subsequent neglect of demonology causes some to overlook the dangers and stop resisting demons. The biblical material on demons, including the descriptions of their abilities and the extent of their powers, should press us into action. A proper understanding

---

29. Lenski states, "From the work of Jesus, Matthew takes us to the motive that lay back of all this work, the Lord's great compassion." Lenski, *Interpretation of St. Matthew's Gospel*, 382.

30. Craig L. Blomberg, *Matthew*, New American Commentary (Nashville: B & H, 1992), 166.

31. Calvin, *Institutes*, Book 1, XIV, Section 19, 155–56.

of demonology should mobilize Christians by encouraging them into faithful living and heartfelt evangelism.

Second, a robust demonology can help train and motivate us to show compassion to the lost. While we are often quick to brand sinners as obstinate and twisted, the reality of demonic activity and their power over the religious and national structures of this world should remind us that Satan has oppressed and blinded those who are without Jesus. They need mercy in keeping with the ministry of Christ. As Jesus delivered us from the chains of the enemy, we are now agents tasked with helping others find freedom and release from bondage to sin in the dominion of demons.[32]

Third, demonology warns us against the dangers of syncretism, universalism, and occultism. Demons are investing their remaining time in deceiving humanity and extending their global rule that is counter to Christ. But other religious and occult beliefs and practices should have no attraction to us. We cannot dare to consider them harmless! Biblical teachings about the demonic underscore the real threat of cultic systems. In the words of Paul to the Galatians, "But now that you have come to know God, or rather to be known by God, how is it that you turn back again to the weak and worthless elementary principles, to which you want to be enslaved all over again?" (Gal 4:9).[33] May we who know the true God never return to our old overlords through syncretism or occultism, nor affirm or accept them through universalism. Let the old gods be dead to us.

---

32. We should also briefly remark upon the phenomenon that in cases of apparent demonic oppression, women tend to be afflicted more than men. Against the backdrop of primarily male leadership in the church, this issue can exacerbate a perception of gender superiority, where men must assist women. While caution is required, let us also remember that demonic powers tend to prey upon the vulnerable and powerless. In many societies, those people are predominantly (and regrettably) women and children. Thus, in some ways we should anticipate the phenomenon, and empower women to counsel and assist other women.

33. Commenting on his passage, Timothy George says,

> All of this has happened to the Galatians by the grace of God, and yet they were in danger of subjecting themselves to a bondage similar to that from which they had been delivered. But how could this be? Had the Galatians actually renounced their Christian faith? Had they recanted their baptismal vows? Did they no longer believe that Jesus was the promised Messiah? Certainly not! The temptation they faced, prompted by the Judaizing false teachers, was to doubt that Jesus Christ *alone* was sufficient for salvation. They were being told that it was necessary to add to their faith in Christ circumcision and other outdated ceremonies of the Mosaic law. Yet to do this, Paul said, would be no different than succumbing to their former subservient obedience to the elemental spirits of the world.

Timothy George, *Galatians*, New American Commentary (Nashville: B & H, 1994), 315, emphasis original.

Fourth, demonology exalts and glorifies Christ in the hearts of the redeemed, leading to worship. The false gods who ruled us, the demons who harassed us, the powers who seemed invincible – all suffered a resounding defeated by the pierced hands of Jesus. Christians should be thoroughly convinced of the loving compassion of God seen in the picture of the cross. And they should be fully aware of his matchless power displayed through his defeat of the demonic host. When human and spiritual opposition demoralize us, biblical demonology reminds us of the just power of God. Demons are defeated creatures, and the wrath of God has set a boundary upon them. They and the other evils of this age will persist only for a little while. In every trial and season, we can exalt Christ as the power above all others.

However, one issue again demands attention as we consider the practicality of demonology. Just as exclusivism is a soteriological outworking of demonology, evangelism is likewise a practical outworking of demonology. With the demonic as the backdrop, evangelism is an operational extension of exclusivism, and Christian salvation supplies us with defenses against the demonic. Freedom is found in Christ, while those outside of Christ are bound by sin and death.

While Jesus Christ is certainly the author and finisher of salvation, his redeemed people are his agents of reconciliation – proclaimers of the gospel message. Evangelism is at the core of Jesus's soteriological purposes, and he involves the redeemed in his saving mission among the nations. If Christ is only the way to God, then those who cling to their own religions stand separated from the true God. Therefore, all religions are not equal. The church must proclaim the message about Jesus to all peoples and declare the way of deliverance from demonic, spiritual bondage.

Yes, Jesus came to set people free. Yet while the atonement is complete, he never intended to act alone in spreading his message and growing his kingdom. "The unreached people of his world need more preachers and ministers of the gospel. Jesus can personally encounter only a small number, so he will commission his followers to begin to reach the rest."[34] The compassionate ministry of the kingdom personally involved Jesus's disciples, and his sending activity culminated at the Great Commission – the conclusion to Matthew's gospel. May we have a heartfelt affection to pour out the gospel and compassionate service on the unconverted. Let us work to help break Satan's shackles of sin from the peoples.

With these practical applications in mind, how can we simply neglect the biblical portrayal of the demonic? By avoiding or denigrating demonology,

---

34. George, *Galatians*, 315.

theological and pastoral deficiencies result. Christ's victory over the demonic is not only a triumph on paper; it empowers each Christian's triumph and ministry in life.

Multicultural Sensitivity

Evangelicals ought to uphold a robust yet restrained demonology, and this balance may encourage better relationships within the contemporary sociological phenomenon of multicultural society – many cultures inhabiting and integrating within the same space. This social phenomenon is a growing norm across the globe. If we compromise, omit, or overemphasize demonology, Christianity can quickly fall into treacherous waters.

First, if we omit demonology or treat it as an unimportant subject, we can harm relationships in multicultural Christian communities including churches, seminaries, and parachurch organizations. A dismissive posture risks alienating Christians who have experiences and cultural backgrounds that support the reality of the demonic. As Ferdinando says, "Most peoples, for most of history, have believed in spirits, witchcraft and sorcery," and since the Scriptures refer to the activity and reality of those spirits, we should not shy away from the subject.[35]

Second, if we compromise our demonology and repackage it according to a cultural philosophy, we communicate a message of arrogance. Instead of the Bible speaking, one culture takes precedence over others. This attitude is catastrophic when attempting to establish and maintain healthy multicultural unity among believers. One common example is how Majority World believers discover an unbiblical hollowness when they join a church with Western roots. Little teaching, if any, is provided concerning demons, and whatever is shared about the demonic is sanitized and minimized so as to not disturb the Western worldview's focus on the physical world. But when a crisis arises from the unseen world, many will pursue counsel from elsewhere, instead of seeking assistance from their own church.

Third, if we overemphasize demons by sensationalizing and exalting their influence in the world, we risk transforming the Christian theology of triumph over the demonic into a pagan dualism – a form of Manichaeism. We could invalidate the holy Christian community itself, creating a dogma that does not represent the Scriptures. While retaining outward forms and terms, Christianity could disappear into the haze of pagan preoccupation and overemphasis on the

---

35. Ferdinando, *Triumph of Christ*, 376.

spirits. For example, one striking church practice in Zambia is the corporate time of simultaneous prayer, wherein everyone speaks or shouts to God as a way to seek deliverance. Whole deliverance services are commonplace, with this form of prayer being a norm! It is even more striking to hear the prayers. "I bind the spirit of joblessness" is a frequent declaration. While a demon could theoretically put someone out of a job (a spirit certainly hurt King Saul's job performance), the job-seeking millions of the world are not likely dealing with demons of joblessness. In this example of prayer and deliverance, African Traditional Religion's concept of the spirits is involved, and it is elevating the influence of demons beyond biblical bounds. Conrad Mbewe begs that we keep the "Trojan Horse outside the gate," for a preoccupation on deliverance practices smuggles animism and syncretism into the church.[36]

In contrast to these lesser options, a biblically derived demonology respects multicultural Christian communities. With the Bible held high, every Christian from every culture can join hands, trusting that God's view of the demonic prevails and that no culture exerts supremacy. Rather, adherence to a biblical demonology will sift every cultural and religious perspective, producing areas of continuity, where Scripture affirms cultural paradigms, and discontinuity, where Scripture revises cultural paradigms.

The Bible sets the proper foundation for theologizing in the multicultural context, especially for demonology which is often a culturally conditioned subject. In our demonology, we must not attempt to insert our own cultural framework into Christianity. Rather, we must try to represent the scriptural material, and use it both to rebuke and affirm our cultural beliefs. If we wish to be sensitive and encouraging to the multicultural Christian community, we must present a truly *biblical* demonology.

What is the purpose of theologizing concerning the demonic? For some of us, the questions and answers are obvious. Biblical teaching on demons is food for the hungry, especially for those of us who need and use a demonological paradigm (good or bad) every day. But what about the rest of us? Perhaps reading this book is your first venture into demonology, having never thought about the subject. We must all grasp demonology and familiarize ourselves with the biblical contours of the doctrine. Otherwise, our view of Scripture slips, our picture of salvation blurs, our framework of ministry neglects, and our intertwined weave of multicultural church unwinds.

---

36. Conrad Mbewe, "A Trojan Horse in The African Church: Deliverance Ministry," *The Gospel Coalition Africa* (12 January 2021).

9

The Challenges to a Demonology for the Global Church

Theological and philosophical diversity are perhaps two of the defining attributes of our time. The societies of the globe are slowly gathering the host of independent intellectual entities into one interconnected whole with billions of voices. Among those voices, one does not need to search hard to discover a variety of perspectives on demonology. Even works like *Understanding Spiritual Warfare: Four Views* fail to encompass all of the options, as the book does not represent authors we have mentioned such as Barth, Unger, Ferdinando, Heiser, and Kato.

In producing a demonology, we have attempted to enter this crowded field by aiming to offer one that avoids cultural leadership and represents the canonical revelation. Unlike others, we have focused on the actions of demons described in Scripture, and we have considered the multicultural ramifications for such a demonology. So what challenges have critics raised against this field of study in general and against this approach in particular? Let us examine five objections concerning our portrayal of the demonic.

The Challenge of "Global"

It is not difficult to anticipate the potential criticisms of this book. Some may lament that it downplays the ancient Near East influence upon biblical depictions of the demonic.[1] Others will object to the synthetization of a unified canonical demonology by asserting that more than one "demonology" exists in

---

1. Considering the relationship of demonic powers to religious systems, we should be exceptionally careful to not treat ancient Near Eastern religious materials as trustworthy witnesses concerning the demonic.

the Bible. While those responses are important, the higher bibliology espoused in our criteria denies that two conflicting demonologies can simultaneously exist in divine revelation and posits the principle of progressive revelation. And thus, our bibliology helps us avoid lengthy tangential wrangling.

Perhaps the most valid criticisms will be about bias, context, and culture. Can any project like this be truly "global" when a man who grew up in the woods of eastern Canada is at the helm? Good point! How can this book be for other places and cultures when it speaks in English by someone conditioned by Western culture and biases? A fair objection.

Ngati mufuna kuziwa zambili, nkala monga simuziwa. This Chewa proverb roughly translates as, "If you want to know much, live like you do not know."[2] I freely confess that I am not the best person to contextualize a demonology into rural Indonesia, urban Moscow, or coastal Brazil. Even after years on the continent of Africa learning from its academics, I am not African, nor do I think in a manner similar to Africans. Demons inhabit, but I do not know the common routes to inhabitation in your area. Demons deceive, but I do not know the common deceptions they use in your culture and local religions.

This book does not presume to solve vexing contextualization issues, which are increasingly complex in our age. Rather, the pages intend to present the biblical material with clarity – not free from bias, but perhaps with a friendly bias – that multicultural and monocultural communities can continue to face the contextualization challenges themselves. I submit this volume with the hope that it may serve the global church with revelatory grounding.

If you contract with a delivery service to get a package, they bring the parcel to your door or gate. Do they enter your home and instruct you how to use the contents in your context? Usually not! In this book, we trust that we have delivered the doctrine, but the contextualization task, how you incarnate and utilize this doctrine in your language and culture remains for your Christian community to determine.

The Challenge of Skepticism

Why believe in unseen demonic beings at all? Many skeptics harshly dismiss the "unenlightened" idea that the spirits and demons of the biblical narratives are real beings. Rodger Bufford, the author of *Counseling and the Demonic*, outlines two common beliefs about the demonic. "According to the first view, demons are everywhere. Those who believe this are preoccupied with demons

---

2. ChiChewa and its dialects is a regional language throughout Malawi and Zambia.

and with efforts to appease, avoid, or escape them. The second view discounts demons, looking on them as irrelevant, at best, or even as nonexistent. Both of these views are mistaken."[3] He goes on to assert that the second view seems "prevalent in Western culture at the present time."[4]

Such an outright denial is difficult within Christian theological circles because Satan and demons are included in the biblical literature. Skeptics take another approach, discarding the reality of personal demons and redefining them as "forces." While we will not repeat the prior discussion of the works of Schleiermacher and Barth, a brief look at Hendrik Berkhof's *Christ and the Powers* will be helpful.

To begin with, Berkhof deserves commendation for treating these demons with seriousness. While others ignore them, he does not. Instead, Berkhof looks at the background of Paul's powers theology (e.g. Eph 1:21; 6:12; Rom 8:38), citing texts like Daniel 10 as important precursors.[5] Paul's powers language did not arise in a vacuum. Berkhof admits that these powers are classified as demons in Jewish thought and that they were "always" classified as personal, spiritual beings.[6] But when he approaches Paul's treatment of the subject, Berkhof moves away from this idea, identifying these beings as earthly power structures, even as he says that "the language of 1 Corinthians 2:8 is more personal."[7] Berkhof plainly states, "One can even doubt whether Paul conceived of the powers as personal beings."[8]

Yes, Berkhof addresses the subject of the powers, but he couches it in rhetoric of doubt and skepticism. He minimizes key contextual points from the canon and from Paul himself to synthesize a world power construct that is not completely controlled by malevolent spiritual beings. And so Berkhof "sets aside the thought that Paul's Powers are angels" and advocates that they are an impersonal element of God's universe.[9] But all of this argumentation is neatly remedied by the close usage of "powers" and "spiritual forces of wickedness in the heavenly places" in Ephesians 6:12. In his commentary on this passage, Lincoln says:

---

3. Rodger K. Bufford, *Counseling and the Demonic* (Dallas: Word, 1988), 11.
4. Bufford, *Counseling and the Demonic*, 12.
5. Hendrik Berkhof, *Christ and the Powers* (Scottdale, PA: Herald, 1977), 16.
6. Berkhof, *Christ and the Powers*, 16–17.
7. Berkhof, 23.
8. Berkhof, 24.
9. Berkhof, 26.

> This verse, which sets out the nature of the enemy, explains further why it is that believers need the divine armor if they are to stand. The spiritual and cosmic nature of the opposition makes such armor absolutely necessary. This is the only place in the Pauline corpus where believers are explicitly said to be in a battle against evil spirit powers. . . . In conformity with the contemporary worldview, the writer depicts human existence as under the influence of powers that work evil.[10]

Paul was referring to spiritual beings under the command of Satan, and we will never know exactly how much skepticism contributed to Berkhof's conclusions. But for certain we can claim that skepticism is the foe of demonology, yet the Bible defends the reality and literal personhood of demons.

The Challenge of Empiricism and Anti-Supernaturalism

What is the source of much of this skepticism? It is empiricism, which is defined as, "The philosophical theory that all ideas are derived from experience, asserting that internal and external experience is the sole foundation of true knowledge and of science."[11] The elevation of experience as a primary criterion for knowledge can prove disastrous for biblical study.[12] Without the repeated performance and verification of a miracle, why would one believe that miracles can occur? In contrast to empiricism, a biblical worldview is dependent on accepting divine revelation as the supreme source of knowledge which grants order and meaning to all other truth.

Demonology is exceptionally vulnerable to mishandling in an experience-dominant perspective. Especially in a culture where people dismiss or redefine demonic actions, the reality of demons and the supernatural in general is questionable. When we are discussing invisible spiritual beings of great power and evil, it is no surprise that an empiricist, who looks for experience as evidence, responds with doubt.

How should we answer such responses? First, we should highlight the experiences of Christians from other cultures and backgrounds. For those who

---

10. Lincoln, *Ephesians*, 443.

11. D. A. Rausch, "Empiricism, Empirical Theology," in *Evangelical Dictionary of Theology*, ed. Walter A. Elwell (Grand Rapids: Baker Book House, 1984), 353.

12. Can anyone empirically determine that all knowledge must be empirically verified? The demand for empirical evidence as the exclusive means to determine truth is self-defeating. Empiricism is not the sole source and arbiter of knowledge.

emphasize experience, we must listen to many sources rather than rushing to our own private conclusions. Multicultural Christian communities are an asset in this endeavor.

Second, empiricists must recognize the unusual category of beings under debate. If someone were to assume a purely physical framework for discerning the reality of a physical object, one could presume a helpful outcome, though still flawed in some senses. But the idea of using natural observation and experience to determine the reality of a supernatural class of malevolent beings seems destined to fail from the outset. In the field of demonology, a bare empiricism is prejudicial, an unfair starting point.

Third, we can point to the fact that limited empirical data for demons does exist. While no one has a caged demon available for testing, an unwise expectation for the study of supernatural beings, personal and cultural accounts of experiences with them abound. Of course, anecdotal evidence is notoriously troublesome, but when a substantial quantity of evidence for demons exists and spans continents, cultures, and centuries, we owe it some credence. Christian demonologists and counselors who specialize in this field, including Bufford, Koch, and Dickason, are not worthy of our ignorance. To those who desire experiments to provide evidence, Koch retorts, "spontaneous occurrences provide more powerful evidence than experiments."[13] And when we are considering the reality of the supernatural demonic beings, we should expect spontaneous interactions rather than the carefully controlled outcomes confined within a repeatable experiment.

While Christian demonology cannot address all the concerns and skepticism of empiricists, revelation and the many observations and experiences we do possess are satisfactory for reasonable dialogue. Enough natural evidence exists to confirm the existing belief in biblical revelation on demons, but that evidence cannot convince on its own.

The Challenge of Speculation and Sensationalism

Excessive and baseless speculation has plagued demonology. While often well-meaning, the result of such overblown curiosity is a demonology that no longer represents the biblical material and its emphases. The reality is this: The Bible is not predominantly concerned with developing a systematized demonology. Nor are demons central characters! Not every narrative, poem, and epistle

---

13. Kurt E. Koch, *Occult ABC* (Grand Rapids: Kregel, 1986), 2.

interact with this field of study. Therefore, the text must restrain a faithful demonology, lest we wander into needless and unsubstantiated speculation.

As an illustration, let us examine William Shackleford's work *Replacing the Fallen Angels*. Consider this excerpt from the opening of his first chapter.

> The origin of choice was not in the perfect will of God though choice began in heaven. Satan developed and exercised choice in heaven strictly against the will of God. The result of his choice was war with God and His faithful angels in heaven, ejection from heaven and a sentence of death to be carried out at some point in the future. . . .
>
> Why did God not destroy Satan and his followers on the spot? He could have very easily. It appears that God reviewed quickly the effect of choice on individual angels. He reviewed the sentence of death for those angels who rebelled and replacing them with more created beings for heaven. As God reviewed all of His options, He developed a plan to give the replacements for the fallen angels [i.e. humans] a choice before He places them in their eternal positions and responsibilities in His kingdom.[14]

In summary, Satan and his angels rebelled against God, and God decided to replace these demonic rebels with redeemed humans who are prepared for the presence of God.

To comment kindly, we commend this hypothesis for its imagination but oppose it for its speculative qualities. Such inventiveness surely runs afoul of our criterion of historical and biblical fidelity. The Scriptures never articulate nor support Shackleford's argument, which is outside the biblical message about the demonic and salvation. Though Jesus does say that resurrected human beings "neither marry nor are given in marriage, but are like angels in heaven," this statement refers exclusively to the end of marital responsibilities (Matt 22:30). Hagner asserts,

> There will be no marriage in the resurrected order. Jesus' answer here must depend on supernatural knowledge. The concluding clause . . . "but they will be like the angels in heaven," must not be generalized to mean altogether or in every respect. The only point made here is that so far as marriage (and sex?) is concerned, human beings will be like the angels, i.e., not marrying.[15]

---

14. William A. Shackleford, *Replacing the Fallen Angels* (Kearney, NE: Morris, 2000), 3.
15. Donald A. Hagner, *Matthew 14–28* (Dallas: Word, 1995), 641.

Shackleford's idea extends beyond the intention of the text, for the context indicates that Jesus was commenting specifically on marriage, not the replacement of fallen angels. At a glance, it makes sense, but it is speculative.

What forms many of our conceptions concerning demons today, in many parts of the world? Movies. And as directors seek to sell tickets and fit the horror genre, sensationalism inevitably follows, even infecting Christians. Summarizing Francesco Bamonte's article from the Vatican newspaper, the Catholic Herald laments:

> Movies depicting exorcisms could be an important medium for showing how God always triumphs over evil, but instead, they misrepresent the faith and exaggerate human and satanic powers over God. . . .
> While there are many inaccuracies about the faith in films, their most serious error is presenting life as a battle between two equal principles or divinities: light and darkness, good and evil.[16]

Thus, while these movies might lead some to dismiss demonization and exorcism as fiction, others will buy into the sensational and exaggerated depictions of demons.

What should we do with speculation and sensationalism, offered by Shackleford and others? We cannot simply refute them with Scripture, since often the Bible does not directly comment. Rather, we must expose the groundlessness of the speculation and sensationalism, having no stable footing in the word of God, and return to biblical themes and emphases.

The Challenges of Ancient Near East (ANE) Culture and Second Temple Judaism

Speculative additions into biblical demonology come from other sources as well. To maintain the centrality of the biblical canon and the sufficiency of its testimony concerning the demonic, we must tread carefully to ensure that the doctrines of culture, both recent and ancient, do not ensnare us. As we look back in history, we could assume that the Hebrew and Greek Scriptures merely reflect the dominant cultural demonologies of their times and locations. Rather, the Bible shows itself accurate in its modesty and consistency by avoiding the speculative tendencies of its historical neighbors and commentators.

---

16. "Exorcism Films Exaggerate Satanic Powers Over God, Says Exorcist," *Catholic Herald* (13 January 2016).

In a recent work, Heiser attempts to recover Christian demonology from its wanderings.

> To be blunt, Christians embrace a number of unbiblical ideas about the power of darkness. The reasons are twofold and are related. First, most of what we claim to know about the powers of darkness does not derive from close study of the original Hebrew and Greek texts. Second, much of what we think we know is filtered through and guided by church tradition – not the original, ancient contexts of the Old and New Testament.[17]

What a laudable pursuit! And in many ways, he rightly corrects common assumptions which persist among God's people. Granting demonology the significance and study it requires, Heiser's research has assisted this volume as well. His laborious analysis of the literature and contexts of the ancient Near East and Second Temple Judaism sheds light on many biblical passages which are fraught with interpretive dangers. However, in some cases, Heiser's efforts to detach demonology from church traditions can lead to an extra-biblical attachment to ancient cultural traditions. Let us examine a few issues.

Disembodied Giants

According to Heiser, the world fell into evil by following the instruction of the *apkallu*, the Mesopotamian term for angelic/semi-divine beings who assisted human civilization before and after the flood.[18] This idea is also reflected in 1 Enoch 65:6. These beings preserved the knowledge of pre-flood humanity and subsequently reseeded it. Heiser correlates the pre-flood *apkallu* with the sons of God of Genesis 6:1–4 and the post-flood *apkallu* with the Nephilim – somewhat human, somewhat angelic.[19] These are the "unclean" or "mixed" offspring of angels and human women. According to his perspective, the Nephilim are the warrior-giants of old. And from where do the demons originate? They are not rebellious spirits from the heavenlies; they are the spirits of the dead giants.[20]

We must agree that the Bible does affirm an angelic invasion into pre-flood humanity. Without embracing the *apkallu* tale, we can certainly affirm that

---

17. Heiser, *Demons*, xv.
18. Heiser, 115–22.
19. Heiser, 121–22.
20. Heiser, 139.

supernatural powers do spread their doctrines. The New Testament verses of 2 Peter 2:4 and Jude 6–7 do also confirm that some angels abandoned their place and sinned in a sexual manner. For this wickedness, God imprisoned that group of angels.

But does the canon confirm that the angelic incursion in Genesis 6 resulted in half-angel offspring? No. The Bible does not portray the Nephilim, the Rephaim, and the Anakim in this manner. The text ascribes nothing additional to them, other than that they are human giants!

> There [in the land of Canaan] also we [Israelite spies] saw the Nephilim (the sons of Anak are part of the Nephilim); and we became like grasshoppers in our own sight, and so we were in their sight.[21]
>
> For only Og king of Bashan was left of the remnant of the Rephaim. Behold, his bedstead was an iron bedstead; it is in Rabbah of the sons of Ammon. Its length was nine cubits and its width four cubits by ordinary cubit.[22]

To reach an angelic conclusion, we must assume and bring in ancient mythology and commentary, from ancient Near East religions that were managed by demons (Deut 32:17) or intertestamental authors that were influenced by those religious tales. The Scriptures themselves never depict demons as the spirits of dead giants.

As we seek a biblical demonology upon which we can confidently rely, Genesis 6 says what it says and no more. Second Peter and Jude support Genesis 6 but not what is contained in Jubilees or 1 Enoch. The New Testament references only affirm the existence of spirits before the flood who sinned, not the reality of human/angel hybrids after the flood. Instead, post-flood

---

21. Numbers 13:33. Cole says,
    Focusing fearfully upon the outward feasibility in the face of the world's power rather than upon their inward faith in God's omnipotence, [the Israelites] lost perspective of the boundless possibilities that awaited them. Suddenly all of the peoples of the land were acclaimed to be like that limited group of descendants of the Anakim who were abnormally large. They began to see themselves as lowly insects, as grasshoppers to be stepped upon on the ground or pinched from the stalks of the fields of the land, to be easily beaten by those inhabitants like the giant Nephilim. Like the later Israelites who trembled before the colossal Goliath and the Philistines, until a devoted youth named David stepped forth to answer the challenge, the Israelites saw themselves being consumed rather than being conquerors through their God.

    R. Dennis Cole, *Numbers*, New American Commentary (Nashville: B & H, 2000), 224.
22. Deuteronomy 3:11.

Scripture depicts heaven as filled with spirits, including malevolent actors (Job 1–2; 1 Kgs 22) who can operate on earth. Why would we assume the ancient cultural position concerning the origins of demons when (1) the Bible does not describe it and (2) the Bible depicts another reasonable explanation – that demons are fallen angels? If the Lord's angels are "ministering spirits" to "those who inherit salvation" (Heb 1:14), why would we not then discern that Satan's angels (as they are labeled in Matt 25:41) are the wicked spirits that work among us on Earth? After all, Satan did inhabit Judas (Luke 22:3)! If we follow the pattern of our work (activity before identity), the conclusion is straightforward: rebellious angels operate as the demonic, unclean spirits.

Behemoth

Heiser also discusses what he calls "demythologized pseudo-demons." Granting too much interpretive control to ancient culture and following 1 Enoch 60, Heiser arrives at a conclusion about the Behemoth that does not fit with the context of Job 40:

> The human plight meant depending on the very thing that could kill you in hundreds of ways. Scholars describe this situation and its biblical expression with terms like "chaos." . . .
>
> Biblical writers framed this situation in light of their belief in God's sovereign control and the involvement of evil spirits in the threats they faced. The metaphor of violent, untamed monsters was common in both biblical and ancient Near Eastern literature. These chaos beasts hailed from the sea (Leviathan, Rahab) and land (Behemoth). . . .
>
> These monsters were not considered real animals one could encounter with unfathomably large dimensions and powers.[23]

In ancient Near East tradition, these beasts were meant to picture the unruly and overwhelming power of unseen and unexplainable spiritual powers. And led by that ancient cultural depiction of such beasts as metaphors for chaos, one might quickly brand Job 40–41 as simply an extension of this pattern.

But Job communicates metaphor and more. The previous chapters describe features of God's creation, and after a brief interjection of God questioning Job, Job 40:15 returns to God's creative work. "Behold, Behemoth, which I made as

---

23. Heiser, 32–33. See pages 170–71 for Heiser's interaction with 1 Enoch 60.

well as you; He eats grass like an ox."[24] Two facts are immediately evident: God created the Behemoth, like Job, and it eats grass. Yes, an allusion to cultural depictions of chaos beasts is probably present, but we should not reduce this passage to only metaphor based upon ancient culture. God is also daring Job to inspect a real animal that he may have encountered. Again, this misstep is no threat to essential Christian doctrine, yet an overreading of cultural context into the text itself can obscure what the dialogue between God and Job says. This monster was real, and it could be encountered.

While historical context can and should assist us, especially in seeing God's triumph over the ancient pseudo-demonic chaos beast metaphor, we must be careful not to let that context lead us in assuming that the beast of Job 40 is not also more than a metaphor, a real beast that could be examined. Biblical demonology is not the culmination of the pneumatatology of the ancient Near East but a repudiation of the demonological systems of that time, and in many ways, Heiser reaches that conclusion. Canonical demonology starkly contrasts against the backdrop of Jubilees and 1 Enoch.

Jubilees and 1 Enoch should not be the grounds upon which we build our demonology. Those works share numerous details that could not possibly be known centuries afterward apart from divine revelation, and if they were divine revelation, they would be canon. For instance, Noah prays in Jubilees 10:3. Why would we assume, millennia after the event, that the recording of the prayer is reliable without divine inspiration? We exhibit skepticism toward Gnostic works attributed to Apostles. Can we then accept Jubilees and 1 Enoch (which is overtly pseudepigraphical) as trustworthy guides for understanding divine revelation concerning the demonic? No. The ancient witnesses are a mixed lot, a concoction of loose references to the Old Testament, extravagant interpretation, and cultural influences. And the form and restraint of the New Testament, though it utilizes some similar terms, is in no way an outright embrace of Second Temple interpretation. It even outright conflicts in places, for 1 Enoch has a plurality of "satans," while the New Testament depicts one

---

24. "This solidly constructed beast is the *first of God's ways* (cf. Prov. 8:22), i.e., the crown of the animal creation. Because Yahweh is *its Maker*, its power and greatness do not exist in opposition to him. In contrast to mythical thought Yahweh did not have to defeat Behemoth to gain control over the forces of chaos. Rather Behemoth obeyed him from the first moment of its origin. In addition, its imposing form bears witness to the majesty of its Creator. Unafraid, Yahweh *can approach* Behemoth *with his sword*. Such an act symbolizes his complete mastery of this beast." Hartley, *The Book of Job*, 525, emphasis original.

alone who is called "Satan."[25] In sum, extra-biblical context can help, but it cannot lead.

An Illustration

Let us propose an example. If we wanted to understand the life of Jesus, we could seek out numerous resources, including the canonical gospels, along with the testimonies contained in the remainder of the New Testament. But they are selective, saying little about the time between the infancy and baptism of Jesus. Yet, supposedly Christian and non-Christian sources have something to offer. The Infancy Gospel of Thomas, along with Surah 5:110 of the Qur'an, recounts the story of the sparrows.

> This little child Jesus when he was five years old was playing at the ford of a brook: and he gathered together the waters that flowed there into pools, and made them straightway clean, and commanded them by his word alone. And having made soft clay, he fashioned thereof twelve sparrows. And it was the Sabbath when he did these things (or made them). And there were also many other little children playing with him.
>
> And a certain Jew when he saw what Jesus did, playing upon the Sabbath day, departed straightway and told his father Joseph: Lo, thy child is at the brook, and he hath taken clay and fashioned twelve little birds, and hath polluted the Sabbath day. And Joseph came to the place and saw: and cried out to him, saying: Wherefore doest thou these things on the Sabbath, which it is not lawful to do? But Jesus clapped his hands together and cried out to the sparrows and said to them: Go! and the sparrows took their flight and went away chirping. And when the Jews saw it they were amazed, and departed and told their chief men that which they had seen Jesus do.[26]

As a child, did Jesus create living sparrows out of clay? It is possible. The content seems similar to biblical material. But how are we supposed to know for sure? The church does not recognize the infancy gospel as canon, and the remaining

---

25. Heiser, *Demons*, 94–95.
26. "The Infancy Gospel of Thomas," *The Gnostic Society Library*, II, 1–5.

contents of the Qur'an are in deep conflict with the Christian faith.[27] In this case, we can neither confirm or deny this tale.

In a similar way, the Bible says little about the historical actions of angels and demons. Genesis 6 speaks a little about the angelic incursion into the human realm, but the text is predominantly setting up for the larger flood narrative. Yet, ancient Near East religious literature and Jewish intertestamental texts fill in the historical blanks. Did fallen angels and human women create a race of giants who then became demons? Theoretically, if there was not canonical reason to reach a different conclusion, it is possible. The content seems similar to biblical material. But how are we supposed to know for sure? The Jewish people did not recognize 1 Enoch or Jubilees as canon, and the remaining contents of ancient Near East religion are in deep conflict with the Torah. In this case, we should remain skeptical.

Can we create a coherent demonology without the leadership of the Ancient Near East culture and Second Temple Judaism? Yes. Will it have a sense of fullness and completion that sates our desire to comprehensively understand the demonic? No, because we cannot fill in the blanks that revelation has left unfilled. Rather, in Scripture, we hold a portrayal of the spiritual realm that is devoid of the sensational and speculative.

We cannot avoid challenges to demonological studies. While we acknowledged the limitations of this effort, we also confronted the ever-present challenges of skepticism, empiricism, speculation, and connections to ancient literature and culture. Yet these challenges manage neither to extinguish the importance of demonology or the reasonableness of the field. And as we reflect on the demonological journey we have taken together – defining criteria, viewing the biblical witness, outlining the purposes, discussing the challenges – we remain with one question: What does the future hold?

---

27. Surah 4:157 rejects that Jesus died on the cross.

10

Demonology for the Global Church in the Days to Come

In this study, we have ventured into the criteria for engaging in demonology. The predominant concern was that the Bible would be central to the study, shaping our demonology by its content and emphases. We cited a consistent hermeneutic as a key criterion in accomplishing this study as well, in order that we may represent the intention of the text, not imposing our own ideas and worldview upon it. We also brought forth the historical Christian perspective on demonology as an asset, even as we sought theological harmony and consistency within our work.

As we transitioned into the content of demonology in the Bible, we prioritized the malevolent activity and speech of demons. We did so by placing this study prior to discussions of their nature. The Scriptures primarily describe the behavior of demons, and we took steps to reflect that emphasis as we detailed various categories for understanding their involvement in the world. Then we summarized their nature status and corporate influence.

But what purpose does demonology serve? We answered that question by stating that demonology upholds the Bible's reliability. It forces us to present a robust soteriology. It supplies crucial practical guidance for Christian living. And a biblical demonology provides the proper soil for the growth of multicultural cooperation and cohesion. In sum, our view of demonology is interwoven with the Bible's reliability and salvation's quality, along with supporting pastoral applications and assisting our growing multicultural Christian communities.

Yet demonology is not without challenges, and after addressing some specific concerns people might have about this book, we responded to general issues that inevitably trouble demonology as a field of study. Especially in the Western world, skepticism reigns concerning the reality and personhood of demons. We also recognized the influence of empiricism in stirring such doubts and anti-supernaturalism. As seen in the example of Shackleford's work, rampant speculation is another challenge. Thankfully, the non-sensationalistic tone and content of the Scriptures answers such attitudes. As we concluded the challenges against demonology, we addressed the temptation to adopt ancient Near East cultural perspectives of the demonic and the speculative interpretations of Second Temple Judaism. While ancient cultural guidance is helpful, we asserted the primacy and infallibility of the canonical witness in defining the boundaries of a dependable demonology.

Where does the study of demonology need to advance in the days to come? It would be foolish to suppose that the matter is finished, especially as the world's societies continue to remake themselves in this globalized era. Here are four thoughts for God's people, whether they be academics, church leaders, or lay people.

Academic Space

After taking a fresh look at the demonology of the Scripture, academics should listen to the testimonies of pastors and deliverance practitioners. Often the temptation is to dismiss these testimonies as the ramblings of uncritical thinkers. But the biblical texts on demons should lead us toward cautious consideration, listening to and dialoguing with the contributions of those who frequently lie outside of the favor of academia.

Years ago, I did not exactly want to study demonology, but by the providence of God, I believed I was led in that direction. But where could I go? Who would supervise such studies? I praise God that I found a professor, the late Gerrit Brand at Stellenbosch University, who was sensitive to the subject even though he and I came from different Christian traditions. When I proposed a study on whether demons are personal beings or not, Brand said, "It reminds me of *The Screwtape Letters*" by C. S. Lewis, and he then encouraged me to move to South Africa. With his guidance, I could study the subject without judgment or disdain, and he pointed me toward various African and European resources.

Academics, are we creating the space necessary to shine light into this dark space? But we should do more than provide room for research! Generations of theologians and pastors across the world have marched through our education curricula without spending any considerable time reflecting on the doctrine of the demonic, which preoccupies the minds of so many lay Christians around the world. We should weep and mourn that our class offerings do not include demonology! We should not wonder why skepticism and speculation abound.

Church Life

Demonology, not only demonological language, has a place within the multicultural church of Jesus Christ. If we truly desire to train well-rounded disciples in the doctrines of the Scriptures, we cannot help but occasionally address the demonic. We must present our response to their vile activities in the context of God's overarching sovereignty.

Two common experiences prevail in the church today, though many variations exist. Some grow up in church hearing doctrine, but this instruction rarely includes anything about demons. Lacking the theological categories to help them comprehend the demonic, these people are then shocked or bewildered when an event occurs which could possibly be demonic. Furthermore, they have trouble bridging the gap with Christians from other backgrounds and experiences.

The other experience is of those who grow up in a church hearing a lot about demons. Family and church leadership have filled their minds with stories about how demons are constantly pestering the church and holding back the blessings of God. Demons are responsible for nearly every sickness, and whenever something tragic takes place, they say, "Satan did this." If someone dares to moderate this point of view with some biblical corrective against sensationalistic claims, especially in a multicultural context, they still struggle to see past Satan and his host as the puppet masters pulling the strings behind all the problems in the world.

The tone and content of the Scriptures are the only medicine for these and other extremes. Can we faithfully deliver the message to raise up Christian communities that are captive to neither ignorance nor excess?

Spiritual Discernment

The path of biblical demonology leads to discernment. While the Bible gives examples of demonic activities, it does not categorically list every scheme and design of Satan and demons through all of history. But a study of the demonic in the Bible should supply us a framework for discernment that we may live wisely. We should not only listen to those involved with these studies, but we should also heed their warnings, lest we act unaware of the enemy's ongoing schemes.

Are we constantly assessing our context and listening to the experiences of others? Since we have an enemy in this world, we must constantly analyze our cultures, religions, practices, and more, seeking discernment from the Spirit in concert with the body of Christ. Guided by the Scriptures, this wisdom can lead to healthy expressions of contextualization.

Missional Importance

The New Testament concept of mission has little in common with the numerous practices that fall under that category of mission today. Mission involves preaching the gospel, discipling believers, training leaders, and planting churches. The book of Acts provides a convincing model of the missions in which Jesus expects his followers to engage.

We cannot state this sentence too forcefully: We have no right to send people on missions, especially in cross-cultural or multicultural contexts, without giving them an understanding of demonology! Since demons are behind the religions of the world and confrontations with those spirits can occur in evangelism, for example as Paul experienced in Philippi, we need people who are entering new contexts to have open eyes to the spiritual dimensions of mission. Are we properly equipping people for the struggles they will encounter? Many missionary sending churches, agencies, and seminaries give minimal instruction on this subject. Thankfully, some missionaries from the Majority World have personal training they can fall back on to counter the lack of formal guidance from various institutions.

In all four of these areas, if we revive the study of biblical demonology, we can look to the future with optimism. Our churches can recover meaningful dialogue and teach doctrine on the demonic in ways that eliminate ignorance and reject excess. We can follow the leadership of academics and clergy who think carefully and biblically on these matters, and we can avoid cultural opinions which will divide our multicultural communities. We can exercise discernment to see the strategies and peculiarities of the influence of demons in our contexts. Our efforts in mission need not be damaged by inexperienced and ill-equipped brothers and sisters. If we desire the health of the global church, demonology is an irreplaceable support to enable it to thrive in the future.

Again, Why Demonology?

Many chapters ago, we asked, "why demonology?" And we discovered that the subject is difficult to avoid, even as we browsed the news. People are talking about the demonic, and many presume that they are encountering these evil beings. But precisely discerning their nature, intentions, and actions is far from straightforward throughout the nations. We – the global church – need to rigorously evaluate our beliefs in light of the biblical witness, and we must protect ourselves from the encroachment of Western philosophical assumptions, as well as speculative cultural perspectives on demons.

Into this world filled with denial and fear of the demonic realm, the Lord speaks through his enlightening word and enables us to understand the world as it is, including the dark powers who seek to deceive and destroy us. Hope displaces fear, chasing the shadows away when we walk in the light of our Savior, Jesus Christ. Biblical demonology answers our pleas for freedom, rescuing us from the pitfalls of our own demonological musings and cultural remedies. Illumining by the Scriptures and the Spirit, Christ still delivers. We need not cower any longer.

Bibliography

Achtemeier, Paul J. *1 Peter: A Commentary on First Peter*. Hermeneia. Minneapolis: Fortress, 1995.
Akin, Daniel L. *1, 2, 3 John*. New American Commentary. Nashville: B & H, 2001.
Alden, Robert L. *Job*. Nashville: B & H, 1993.
Anderson, Neil T., and Timothy M. Warner. *The Beginner's Guide to Spiritual Warfare*. Ann Arbor, MI: Servant, 2000.
Anderson, Troi. "Summoning Spirits in Venezuala." *CNN Photos*, 16 January 2014. https://cnnphotos.blogs.cnn.com/category/troi-anderson/, http://www.troianderson.com/espiritismo-theater-and-trance/.
Arnold, Clinton. "Returning to the Domain of the Powers: Stoicheia as Evil Spirits in Galatians 4:3,9." *Novum Testamentum* 38, no. 1 (1996): 55–76.
Attridge, Harold W., and Helmut Koester. *The Epistle to the Hebrews: A Commentary on the Epistle to the Hebrews*. Hermeneia. Philadelphia: Fortress, 1989.
"The Augsburg Confession – by Philip Melancthon (1497–1560)." *A Puritan's Mind*. https://www.apuritansmind.com/creeds-and-confessions/the-augsburg-confessionby-by-philip-melancthon-1497-1560/.
Augustine. *The City of God against the Pagans*. Edited by R. W. Dyson. Cambridge: Cambridge University Press, 2002.
Baker, Warren, and Eugene Carpenter. *The Complete Word Study Dictionary: Old Testament*. Chattanooga, TN: AMG, 2003.
Barnett, Paul. *The Second Epistle to the Corinthians*. New International Commentary on the New Testament. Grand Rapids: Eerdmans, 1997.
Barth, Karl. *Church Dogmatics*. Translated by G. W. Bromiley and R. J. Ehrlich. Peabody, MA: Hendrickson, 2010.
Bauckham, Richard. "Spirits in Prison." In *The Anchor Bible Dictionary*, edited by D. N. Freedman. New York: Doubleday, 1992.
Beasley-Murray, George R. *John*. Waco, TX: Word, 1987.
Bediako, Kwame. *Jesus and the Gospel in Africa: History and Experience*. New York: Orbis, 2004.
Bergen, Robert D. *1, 2 Samuel*. New American Commentary. Nashville: B & H, 1996.
Berkhof, Hendrik. *Christ and the Powers*. Scottdale, PA: Herald, 1977.
Blomberg, Craig L. *Matthew*. New American Commentary. Nashville: B & H, 1992.
Borchert, Gerald L. *John 1–11*. New American Commentary. Nashville: B & H, 2002.
———. *John 12–21*. New American Commentary. Nashville: B & H, 2002.
Bovon, François, and Helmut Koester. *Luke 1: A Commentary on the Gospel of Luke 1:1–9:50*. Minneapolis: Fortress, 2002.

Brand, Gerrit. *Speaking of a Fabulous Ghost: In Search of Theological Criteria, with Special Reference to the Debate on Salvation in African Christian Theology.* Frankfurt Am Main: P. Lang, 2002.

Bratcher, Robert G., and Howard A. Hatton. *A Handbook on the Revelation to John.* UBS New Testament Handbook Series. New York: United Bible Societies, 1993.

Bratcher, Robert G., and William D. Reyburn. *A Handbook on Psalms.* UBS Old Testament Handbook Series. New York: United Bible Societies, 1993.

Bromiley, G. W. *An Introduction to the Theology of Karl Barth.* Grand Rapids: Eerdmans, 1979.

Brown, Francis, S. R. Driver, and Charles A. Briggs. *A Hebrew and English Lexicon of the Old Testament* (BDB Complete). Dania Beach, FL: Scribe, 2000.

Bruce, F. F. *The Book of the Acts.* New International Commentary on the New Testament. Grand Rapids: Eerdmans, 1988.

———. *The Epistles to the Colossians, to Philemon, and to the Ephesians.* New International Commentary on the New Testament. Grand Rapids: Eerdmans, 1984. *Accordance Electronic Edition.*

Bufford, Rodger K. *Counseling and the Demonic.* Dallas: Word, 1988.

Calvin, John. *Institutes of the Christian Religion.* Translated by Henry Beveridge. Grand Rapids: Eerdmans, 1970.

Cole, R. Dennis. *Numbers.* New American Commentary. Nashville: B & H, 2000.

Collins, John J., Frank Moore Cross, and Adela Yarbro Collins. *Daniel: A Commentary on the Book of Daniel.* Hermeneia. Minneapolis: Fortress, 1993.

Conzelmann, Hans. *Acts of the Apostles: A Commentary on the Acts of the Apostles.* Hermeneia. Minneapolis: Fortress, 1987.

———. *1 Corinthians: A Commentary on the First Epistle to the Corinthians.* Hermeneia. Philadelphia: Fortress, 1975.

Cooper, Lamar Eugene. *Ezekiel.* Nashville: B & H, 1994.

Danker, Frederick W., Walter Bauer, William F. Arndt, and F. Wilbur Gingrich. *Greek-English Lexicon of the New Testament and Other Early Christian Literature* (BDAG). 3rd ed. Chicago: University of Chicago Press, 2000.

Dibelius, Martin, and Hans Conzelmann. *The Pastoral Epistles: A Commentary on the Pastoral Epistles.* Hermeneia. Philadelphia: Fortress, 1972.

Dibelius, Martin, and Heinrich Greeven. *James: A Commentary on the Epistle of James.* Hermeneia. Philadelphia: Fortress, 1976.

Dickason, C. Fred. *Angels, Elect and Evil.* Chicago: Moody, 1975.

Dickson, Kwesi. "African Theology: Origin, Methodology and Content." *The Journal of Religious Thought* 32, no. 2 (1975): 34–45.

Enns, Paul. *The Moody Handbook of Theology.* Chicago: Moody, 2014.

Enroth, R. M. "The Occult." In *Evangelical Dictionary of Theology*, edited by Walter A. Elwell. Grand Rapids: Baker Book House, 1984.

Evans, Craig A. *Mark 8:27–16:20.* Nashville: Thomas Nelson, 2001.

"Exorcism Films Exaggerate Satanic Powers Over God, Says Exorcist." *Catholic Herald.* 13 January 2016. https://catholicherald.co.uk/exorcism-films-exaggerate-satanic-powers-over-god-says-exorcist/

Fee, Gordon D. *The First Epistle to the Corinthians.* New International Commentary on the New Testament. Grand Rapids: Eerdmans, 2014.

———. *The First and Second Letters to the Thessalonians.* New International Commentary on the New Testament. Grand Rapids: Eerdmans, 2009.

Ferdinando, Keith. *The Triumph of Christ in African Perspective: A Study of Demonology and Redemption in the African Context.* Carlisle, UK: Paternoster, 1999.

Ferguson, Everett. *Demonology of the Early Christian World.* New York: E. Mellen, 1984.

Garland, David E. *2 Corinthians.* New American Commentary. Nashville: B & H, 1999.

George, Timothy. *Galatians.* Nashville: B & H, 1994.

Green, Daniel. "Revelation." In *The Moody Bible Commentary*, edited by Michael Rydelnik and Michael Vanlaningham. Chicago: Moody, 2014.

Grudem, Wayne A. *Systematic Theology: An Introduction to Biblical Doctrine.* Grand Rapids: Zondervan, 2000.

Guelich, Robert A. *Mark 1–8:26.* Grand Rapids: Zondervan, 1989.

Haenchen, Ernst, Robert W. Funk, and Ulrich Busse. *John: A Commentary on the Gospel of John.* Hermeneia. Philadelphia: Fortress, 1984.

Hagner, Donald A. *Matthew 1–13.* Dallas: Word, 1993.

———. *Matthew 14–28.* Dallas: Word, 1995.

Hamilton, Victor P. *The Book of Genesis, Chapters 1–17.* New International Commentary on the Old Testament. Grand Rapids: Eerdmans, 1990.

Hartley, John E. *The Book of Job.* New International Commentary on the Old Testament. Grand Rapids: Eerdmans, 1988.

"Haunted House's 'Ghost' Attacks News Crew." *WPMT* (CNN Affiliate), 5 August 2014. http://www.cnn.com/videos/bestoftv/2014/08/05/dnt-pa-news-crew-visits-haunted-house.wpmt.

Heider, G. C. "Molech." In *Dictionary of Deities and Demons in the Bible*, edited by K. Van Der Toorn, Bob Becking, and Pieter Willem Van Der Horst. Leiden: Brill, 1999.

Heiser, Michael S. *Demons: What the Bible Really Says about the Powers of Darkness.* Bellingham, WA: Lexham, 2020.

———. "Deuteronomy 32:8 and the Sons of God." *The Divine Council.* http://www.thedivinecouncil.com/DT32BibSac.pdf.

Hollenweger, W. J. "Intercultural Theology." *Theology Today* 43, no. 1 (1986): 28–35.

House, Paul R. *1, 2 Kings.* New American Commentary. Nashville: B & H, 1995.

"The Infancy Gospel of Thomas." *The Gnostic Society Library.* http://gnosis.org/library/inftoma.htm.

Jewett, Robert K., and Roy D. Kotansky. *Romans: A Commentary on the Book of Romans.* Hermeneia. Minneapolis: Fortress, 2007.

Kato, Byang H. *African Cultural Revolution and the Christian Faith*. Jos, Nigeria: Challenge, 1976.

———. "Contextualization of the Gospel: Theological Perspective." [Typescript] in *Byang H. Kato: 1936-1975: Perspectives of an African Theologian: The Writings of Byang H. Kato Th.D.*, ACTEA Data CD, 2007.

———. *Theological Pitfalls in Africa*. Kisumu, Kenya: Evangel, 1975.

———. *What the Bible Teaches: The Spirits*. Achimota, Ghana: Africa Christian, 1975.

Keener, Craig S. *The IVP Bible Background Commentary: New Testament*. Downers Grove, IL: InterVarsity, 2014.

Klein, George L. *Zechariah*. New American Commentary. Nashville: B & H, 2007.

Koch, Kurt E. *Occult ABC*. Grand Rapids: Kregel, 1986.

Kraft, Charles H. "Culture, Worldview and Contextualization." In *Perspectives on the World Christian Movement*, 384–91. Pasadena, CA: William Carey Library, 1998. http://media2.gracechurchsc.org/wp-content/uploads/2012/04/kraft_culture_worldview.pdf.

"Kristine McGuire: A Ghost Hunter Calls on Christ." *CBN.com, TV and Video*. n.d. http://www.cbn.com/tv/1744351612001.

Kuemmerlin-McLean, Joanne, K. "Demons." In *The Anchor Bible Dictionary*, edited by D. N. Freedman. Vol. 2. New York: Doubleday, 1992.

Lea, Thomas D., and Hayne P. Griffin Jr. *1, 2 Timothy, Titus*. New American Commentary. Nashville: B & H, 1992.

Lenski, R. C. H. *The Interpretation of the Acts of the Apostles*. Minneapolis: Augsburg, 1961.

———. *The Interpretation of St. John's Gospel*. Minneapolis: Augsburg, 1961.

———. *The Interpretation of St. John's Revelation*. Minneapolis: Augsburg, 1963.

———. *The Interpretation of St. Mark's Gospel*. Minneapolis: Augsburg, 1961.

———. *The Interpretation of St. Matthew's Gospel*. Minneapolis: Augsburg, 1961.

———. *The Interpretation of St. Paul's Epistles to the Colossians, to the Thessalonians, to Timothy, to Titus and to Philemon*. Minneapolis: Augsburg, 1961.

———. *The Interpretation of St. Paul's First and Second Epistles to the Corinthians*. Minneapolis: Augsburg, 1963.

———. *The Interpretation of St. Paul's Epistles to the Galatians, to the Ephesians and to the Philippians*. Minneapolis: Augsburg, 1961.

———. *The Interpretation of the Epistles of St. Peter, St. John and St. Jude*. Minneapolis: Augsburg, 1966.

Lincoln, Andrew T. *Ephesians*. Dallas: Word, 1990.

Lutzer, Erwin W. *God's Devil: The Incredible Story of How Satan's Rebellion Serves God's Purposes*. Chicago: Moody, 1996.

Marshall, I. Howard. *The Gospel of Luke: A Commentary on the Greek Text*. New International Greek Testament Commentary. Grand Rapids: Eerdmans, 1978.

Mathews, Kenneth A. *Genesis 1–11:26*. New American Commentary. Nashville: B & H, 1996.

Mayhew, Eugene J. "Job." In *The Moody Bible Commentary*, edited by Michael Rydelnik and Michael Vanlaningham. Chicago: Moody, 2014.
Mbewe, Conrad. "A Trojan Horse in The African Church: Deliverance Ministry." *The Gospel Coalition Africa*. 12 January 2021. https://africa.thegospelcoalition.org/article/a-trojan-horse-in-the-african-church-deliverance-ministry/.
Mbiti, John S. *African Religions and Philosophy*. Portsmouth, NH: Heinemann, 1990.
McKinion, Steven A., ed. *Isaiah 1–39*. Ancient Christian Commentary Series. Downers Grove, IL: InterVarsity, 2004.
Meier, S. A. "Angel I." In *Dictionary of Deities and Demons in the Bible*, edited by K. Van Der Toorn, Bob Becking, and Pieter Willem Van Der Horst. Leiden: Brill, 1999.
Melick, Richard R. *Philippians, Colossians, Philemon*. Nashville: B & H, 1991.
Merrill, Eugene H. *Deuteronomy*. New American Commentary. Nashville: B & H, 1994.
Meyer, Kyle. "Swaziland Church Battles Demons." *CNN Photos*, 19 November 2013. https://cnnphotos.blogs.cnn.com/category/kyle-meyer/, https://visura.co/thekylemeyer/stories/touch-of-god-2.
Migiro, Geoffrey. "The Most Diverse Cities in the World." *WorldAtlas*, 28 March 2019. http://worldatlas.com/articles/the-most-diverse-cities-in-the-world.html.
Miller, Stephen, R. *Daniel*. New American Commentary. Nashville: B & H, 1994.
Moreau, A. Scott. "Contextualization That Is Comprehensive." *Missiology: An International Review* 34, no. 3 (2006): 325–35.
Mounce, Robert H. *The Book of Revelation*. New International Commentary on the New Testament. Grand Rapids: Eerdmans, 1997.
Nadar, Sarojini. "Contextual Theological Education in Africa." *The Ecumenical Review* 59, no. 2–3 (2007): 235–41.
Nevius, John Livingstone. *Demon Possession and Allied Themes*. Memphis: General Books, 1894.
Newsom, Carol A. "Angels." In *The Anchor Bible Dictionary*, edited by D. N. Freedman. Vol. 1. New York: Doubleday, 1992.
"The Nicene Creed Circa 381 A.D." *A Puritan's Mind*. https://www.apuritansmind.com/creeds-and-confessions/nicene-creed/.
Nickelsburg, George W. E., and Klaus Baltzer. *1 Enoch: A Commentary on the Book of 1 Enoch*. Hermeneia. Minneapolis: Fortress, 2001.
"Nigeria Rescues Girls from 'Baby Factory.'" *News24*, 13 April 2012. http://www.news24.com/Africa/News/Nigeria-rescues-girls-from-baby-factory-20120413.
Nolland, John. *Luke 1–9:20*. Nashville: Thomas Nelson, 1989.
———. *Luke 9:21–18:34*. Dallas: Word, 1993.
Nwankpa, Vincent Onyebuchi. *Understanding Cultural Perspectives, God's Word, and Missions: A Powerful Tool for Theologizing*. Bloomington, IN: Authorhouse, 2009.
Ooi, Samuel Hio-Kee. "A Study of Strategic Level Spiritual Warfare from a Chinese Perspective." *Asian Journal of Pentecostal Studies* 9, no. 1 (2006): 143–61.
Oswalt, John. *The Book of Isaiah, Chapters 1–39*. New International Commentary on the Old Testament. Grand Rapids: Eerdmans, 1986.

Payne, Karl I. *Spiritual Warfare: Christians, Demonization, and Deliverance.* Washington, DC: WND, 2011.
Pierard, R. V. "Evangelicalism." In *Evangelical Dictionary of Theology*, edited by Walter A. Elwell. Grand Rapids: Baker Book House, 1984.
Pobee, John S. *Toward an African Theology.* Nashville: Abingdon, 1979.
Polhill, John B. *Acts.* Nashville: B & H, 1992.
Poythress, Vern. "Christ the Only Savior of Interpretation." *Westminster Theological Journal* 50, no. 2 (1988): 305–21.
———. "Divine Meaning of Scripture." *Westminster Theological Journal* 48 (1986): 241–79.
Rausch, D. A. "Empiricism, Empirical Theology." In *Evangelical Dictionary of Theology*, edited by Walter A. Elwell. Grand Rapids: Baker Book House, 1984.
Richardson, Kurt A. *James.* New American Commentary. Nashville: B & H, 1997.
Riley, G. J. "Devil." In *Dictionary of Deities and Demons in the Bible*, edited by K. Van Der Toorn, Bob Becking, and Pieter Willem Van Der Horst. Leiden: Brill, 1999.
Rooker, Mark F. *Leviticus.* New American Commentary. Nashville: B & H, 2000. *Accordance Electronic Edition.*
Schleiermacher, Friedrich. *The Christian Faith.* Edinburgh: T & T Clark, 1928.
Schreiner, Thomas R. *1, 2 Peter, Jude.* New American Commentary. Nashville: B & H, 2003. *Accordance Electronic Edition.*
Schreiter, Robert J. "Multicultural Ministry: Theory, Practice, Theology." *New Theology Review* 5, no. 3 (1992).
Shackleford, William A., Sr. *Replacing the Fallen Angels.* Kearney, NE: Morris, 2000.
Simons, Jake Wallis. "The 'Catholic Witchdoctors' of Bolivia: Where God and Ancient Spirits Collide." *CNN Travel*, 17 September 2014. http://www.cnn.com/2014/09/17/travel/catholic-witchdoctors-of-bolivia/.
Simpson, J. W., Jr. "Spirit." In *The International Standard Bible Encyclopedia*, edited by G. W. Bromiley. Grand Rapids: Eerdmans, 1979. *PC Study Bible Database.*
Smit, Dirk J. "Reading the Bible and the (Un)official Interpretive Culture." *Neotestimentica* 28, no. 2 (1994): 309–21.
Smith, Gary V. *Isaiah 1–39.* New American Commentary. Nashville: B & H, 2007.
Snodgrass, Klyne R. "An Introduction to a Hermeneutics of Identity." *Bibliotheca Sacra* 168 (Jan-Mar, 2011): 3–19.
Song, Sarah. "Multiculturalism." *The Stanford Encyclopedia of Philosophy Archive*, Spring 2017 Edition. 12 August 2016. https://plato.stanford.edu/archives/spr2017/entries/multiculturalism/.
Stein, Gordon. *The Encyclopedia of the Paranormal.* Amherst, NY: Prometheus, 1996.
Stein, Robert H. *Luke.* New American Commentary. Nashville: B & H, 1992.
Stoddard, Eowyn. "Dealing with Demons." *The Gospel Coalition*, 9 December 2013. http://www.thegospelcoalition.org/article/dealing-with-demons/.
Strecker, Georg, and Harold W. Attridge. *The Johannine Letters: A Commentary on 1, 2, and 3 John.* Hermeneia. Minneapolis: Fortress, 1996.

Stuart, Douglas K. *Exodus*. New American Commentary. Nashville: B & H, 2006.
Summers, Montague, trans. *The Malleus Maleficarum of Heinrich Kramer and James Sprenger*. 1928. Reprint Downers Grove, IL: Dover, 1971.
Tanner, Kathryn. *Theories of Culture: A New Agenda for Theology*. Minneapolis: Fortress, 1997.
Tate, Marvin E. *Psalms 51–100*. Nashville: Thomas Nelson, 2003.
Taylor, Mark. *1 Corinthians*. New American Commentary. Nashville: B & H, 2014.
Tennent, Timothy C. *Theology in the Context of World Christianity: How the Global Church Is Influencing the Way We Think About and Discuss Theology*. Grand Rapids: Zondervan, 2007.
Thompson, J. A. *1, 2 Chronicles*. New American Commentary. Nashville: B & H, 1994.
Towner, Philip H. *The Letters to Timothy and Titus*. New International Commentary on the New Testament. Grand Rapids: Eerdmans, 2006.
Unger, Merrill F. *Biblical Demonology: A Study of the Spiritual Forces behind the Present World Unrest*. Wheaton, IL: Scripture, 1952.
Van Henten, J. W. "Angel II." In *Dictionary of Deities and Demons in the Bible*, edited by K. Van Der Toorn, Bob Becking, and Pieter Willem Van Der Horst. Leiden: Brill, 1999.
Vanhoozer, Kevin J. *The Drama of Doctrine: A Canonical Linguistic Approach to Christian Theology*. Louisville: Westminster John Knox, 2005.
———. *Is There a Meaning in This Text?* Grand Rapids: Zondervan, 1998.
Walton, John H., Victor Harold Matthews, and Mark W. Chavalas. *The IVP Bible Background Commentary: Old Testament*. Downers Grove, IL: InterVarsity, 2000.
"Watch Pastor Perform Exorcisms." *CNN*, 24 January 2014. http://www.cnn.com/videos/living/2014/01/25/ac-pkg-tuchman-reverend-exorcisms.cnn.
"Westminster Larger Catechism." *A Puritan's Mind*. https://www.apuritansmind.com/westminster-standards/larger-catechism/.
White, R. E. O. "Salvation." In *Evangelical Dictionary of Theology*, edited by Walter A. Elwell. Grand Rapids, MI: Baker Book House, 1984.
Wink, Walter. *The Powers That Be: Theology for a New Millennium*. New York: Doubleday, 1998.
Wink, Walter, David Powlison, Gregory Boyd, C. Peter Wagner, and Rebecca Greenwood. *Understanding Spiritual Warfare: Four Views*. Edited by James K. Beilby and Paul R. Eddy. Grand Rapids: Baker Academic, 2012.
Zuck, Roy B. *Basic Bible Interpretation*. Wheaton, IL: Victor, 1991.

Langham Literature and its imprints are a ministry of Langham Partnership.

Langham Partnership is a global fellowship working in pursuit of the vision God entrusted to its founder John Stott –

> *to facilitate the growth of the church in maturity and Christ-likeness through raising the standards of biblical preaching and teaching.*

Our vision is to see churches in the Majority World equipped for mission and growing to maturity in Christ through the ministry of pastors and leaders who believe, teach and live by the word of God.

Our mission is to strengthen the ministry of the word of God through:
- nurturing national movements for biblical preaching
- fostering the creation and distribution of evangelical literature
- enhancing evangelical theological education

especially in countries where churches are under-resourced.

Our ministry

Langham Preaching partners with national leaders to nurture indigenous biblical preaching movements for pastors and lay preachers all around the world. With the support of a team of trainers from many countries, a multi-level programme of seminars provides practical training, and is followed by a programme for training local facilitators. Local preachers' groups and national and regional networks ensure continuity and ongoing development, seeking to build vigorous movements committed to Bible exposition.

Langham Literature provides Majority World preachers, scholars and seminary libraries with evangelical books and electronic resources through publishing and distribution, grants and discounts. The programme also fosters the creation of indigenous evangelical books in many languages, through writer's grants, strengthening local evangelical publishing houses, and investment in major regional literature projects, such as one volume Bible commentaries like *The Africa Bible Commentary* and *The South Asia Bible Commentary*.

Langham Scholars provides financial support for evangelical doctoral students from the Majority World so that, when they return home, they may train pastors and other Christian leaders with sound, biblical and theological teaching. This programme equips those who equip others. Langham Scholars also works in partnership with Majority World seminaries in strengthening evangelical theological education. A growing number of Langham Scholars study in high quality doctoral programmes in the Majority World itself. As well as teaching the next generation of pastors, graduated Langham Scholars exercise significant influence through their writing and leadership.

To learn more about Langham Partnership and the work we do visit **langham.org**

www.ingramcontent.com/pod-product-compliance
Lightning Source LLC
Chambersburg PA
CBHW050811160426
43192CB00010B/1720